TEACHER'S MANUAL
ReadSmart 1
HIGH BEGINNING

Diana Renn

ReadSmart 1 Teacher's Manual, First Edition

Published by McGraw-Hill ESL/ELT, a business unit of The McGraw-Hill Companies, Inc. 1221 Avenue of the Americas, New York, NY 10020. Copyright ©2005 by The McGraw-Hill Companies, Inc. All rights reserved. No part of this publication may be reproduced or distributed in any form or by any means, or stored in a database or retrieval system, without the prior written consent of The McGraw-Hill Companies, Inc., including, but not limited to, in any network or other electronic storage or transmission, or broadcast for distance learning.

This book is printed on recycled, acid-free paper containing 10% postconsumer waste.

1 2 3 4 5 6 7 8 9 QPD 9 8 7 6 5 4

ISBN: 0-07-283892-2

Editorial director: *Tina B. Carver*
Senior sponsoring editor: *Thomas Healy*
Senior developmental editor: *Annie Sullivan*
Editorial assistant: *Kasey Williamson*
Production manager: *MaryRose Malley*
Cover design: *Martini Graphic Services, Inc. Joe Martini*
Interior design: *Martini Graphic Services, Inc. Juan A. Bautista*

Table of Contents

Introduction vi

Student Book Answer Keys vii

Appendices Answer Keys 138

Quizzes 1–6 140

Quiz Answer Keys 166

Introduction

ReadSmart 1 is a high beginning reading skills text for students who are studying English. It is part of the three-book ***ReadSmart*** series. The text consists of thirteen chapters and features extensive reading and vocabulary skills instruction chapters, followed by ample opportunities to practice the target skills. The topics, reading genres, and strategies were purposefully chosen to accommodate a wide variety of students. The themes in the reading chapters were chosen to relate to different academic disciplines, although most of the readings themselves are non-academic in nature. Therefore, the series can be used with students who would like to read more effectively for academic, career, or general purposes.

Student Book Overview

Introductory Chapter

ReadSmart 1 begins with an introductory chapter on the mechanics of reading. This chapter provides practice in the physical skills required for scanning, skimming, and reading more quickly. The exercises focus on things such as rapid eye movement, using your hand to move down the page, and so on.

Skills and Strategies Chapters (1, 5, 9)

There are three **Skills and Strategies chapters** in the text (Chapters 1, 5, and 9). These chapters present skills and strategies for improving your reading. Skills and strategies for comprehension are taught in Part 1; skills and strategies for understanding vocabulary are taught in Part 2. The comprehension section is further divided into steps in the reading process: *Prepare, Read,* and *Remember*. Although **ReadSmart** teaches that reading is not necessarily a linear process, these chapters do teach and practice skills and strategies in a logical progression to ensure that students have mastered them in isolation before applying them.

Each strategy is introduced, explained, and then practiced. The exercises in these chapters are controlled so that students benefit from focused practice of individual skills and strategies. Especially useful strategies, such as using signal words to predict ideas, are taught and recycled in every skills/strategies chapter with different material.

Thematic Reading Chapters (2, 3, 4, 6, 7, 8, 10, 11, 12)

There are nine **Reading chapters** in the text (Chapters 2–4, 6–8, and 10–12). Each reading chapter contains four thematic readings in a variety of genres, including magazine articles, textbook excerpts, Websites, travel brochures, and newspaper articles. The activities accompanying the readings are designed specifically to target the comprehension and vocabulary skills and strategies that students learned in the previous skills/strategies chapter. But rather than provide additional focused practice of individual strategies, the reading chapters ask students to apply the skills and strategies in powerful combinations as they read. As the text progresses, skills and strategies are recycled in the reading chapters naturally.

The reading chapters open with a topical photo and discussion questions. These tools activate students' background knowledge about the topic and prompt them into thinking about the topic in a general way. The four readings in the chapter expand the steps in the reading process: *Prepare, Read, Read Again, Remember,* and *Discuss*.

The comprehension and vocabulary skills and strategies taught in the skills/strategies chapters are embedded in the reading steps. *Post-Reading Activities* focus students' attention more closely on strategies appropriate for each reading.

Thinking About Strategies prompts students to reflect on the strategies that they used in each reading.

Teacher's Manual

This Teacher's Manual provides answers to the activities and questions in the ***ReadSmart 1*** Student Book. Some questions and activities, such as reading comprehension questions, will have definite answers. However, ***ReadSmart 1*** also provides many open-ended questions and activities. For example, students are frequently asked to write questions based on a quick preview of a text, or to guess possible word definitions from context or from analyzing word parts. Therefore, possible answers for more open-ended questions are provided whenever possible in order to help the instructor anticipate student responses.

Quizzes

Six reproducible quizzes, each worth 100 points, are provided in this Teacher's Manual. The quizzes assess student mastery of the skills and strategies presented in the Student Book. The quizzes also increase student competence in following standardized and performance-based test formats. Each quiz begins with a reading passage that links thematically to its corresponding chapters. Questions on reading and vocabulary skills follow each passage. Quiz items ask students to apply the strategies they have learned, and many quiz items follow a similar format to the activities in the Student Book. However, unlike some of the Student Book activities, the quiz items use formats with definite answer choices, allowing for easy scoring. The instructor can use the quizzes to determine how well the students have mastered the skills, and to identify those skills needing further review.

A quiz may be given after every two chapters according to the following schedule:

Quiz	Corresponding Student Book Chapters
Quiz 1	Chapters 1 and 2
Quiz 2	Chapters 3 and 4
Quiz 3	Chapters 5 and 6
Quiz 4	Chapters 7 and 8
Quiz 5	Chapters 9 and 10
Quiz 6	Chapters 11 and 12

Quiz Answer Keys follow the six quizzes in this Teacher's Manual.

The Mechanics of Reading: Scanning and Skimming

Scanning
Student Book p. xii

ACTIVITY 1

1. The word "possible" appears twice.
2. The word "made" appears three times.
3. The word "think" appears twice.
4. The word "night" appears three times.
5. The word "touch" appears three times.
6. The word "tried" appears twice.
7. The word "calm" appears three times.
8. The word "biology" appears twice.
9. The word "peach" appears twice.
10. The word "reading" appears twice.

ACTIVITY 2

1. The word "telephone" appears twice—once with a capital *T*, once with a lowercase *t*.
2. The time "10:32 A.M." appears once.
3. The abbreviation "CO" appears once.
4. The number "1,932" appears once.
5. The temperature "32° C" appears twice.
6. The word "information" does not have a match.
7. The acronym "GSU" appears once.
8. The word "electrical" appears once.
9. The date "March 1" appears once.
10. The number "4,057.89" appears once.

ACTIVITY 3

1. The phrase "practice reading faster" appears seven times.
2. The phrase "the small red brick house" appears four times.

ACTIVITY 4

1. a. The temperature in Cleveland is 72°.
   b. The weather in Miami is rainy.
   c. The coldest city on this day is Denver.
   d. The hottest city on this day is Los Angeles.
2. a. "The Art of Sports Announcing," page 56.
   b. "What Makes a Great Coach," page 108
   c. "A Basketball Legend," page 33.
3. a. Frazier & Son is a furniture store.
   b. The phone number of Green Mountain Interiors is 464-3007.
   c. Furniture Plus opens at 9:00 A.M. Monday through Saturday and 10:00 A.M. on Sunday.
   d. Emerson's Inc sells Englander mattresses.
4. a. An avalanche contains ice, soil, rocks, and even trees.
   b. The avalanche happened on Mount Sanford in Alaska.
   c. An avalanche can move as quickly as 245 miles an hour.

Skimming
Student Book p. 6

ACTIVITY 5

The best title for the article is (b) *Looking for Fun? Go to Hamburger Heaven.*

ACTIVITY 6

The best title for the article is (b) *Animals Found Buried with Egyptian Mummies.*

CHAPTER 1

ACTIVITY 7

The best title for the article is (a) *Why is a Résumé Important?*

ACTIVITY 8

The best title for the article is (b) *The Benefits of Bicycling.*

Reading Skills and Strategies

Prepare

Making Predictions about the Text
Student Book p. 9

ACTIVITY 1

For the article "Kicking the Cigarette Habit," the topic is probably quitting smoking with your partner.

For the textbook chapter from *Earth Sciences*, the topic is probably layers of vegetation or plant life beneath the earth's surface.

Exploring What You Already Know
Student Book p. 12

Understanding the Strategy

Answers may vary. Possible answers:

1. The topic is five steps to buying a very good CD player. To "purchase" something means to buy it. The five steps might be researching the products online, talking to friends or other people about the product, looking at CD players in stores, evaluating prices, and buying the CD player.

2. Possible brainstormed ideas:
   - Before buying a CD player or other items, you might check brand names, features, and prices and compare them with other products.
   - You might talk to friends about what they have bought or what they would recommend.
   - You might research the product on the Internet or in a magazine.
   - In the store, you might talk with a sales clerk to get more information and to be sure you are making a good choice. You might compare brands or prices with similar products while in the store.

3. Possible notes (facts or memories recalled from an experience of purchasing something like a CD player):
   - Friend told me that you get what you pay for—he bought a cheap CD player, but it broke the first time he used it.
   - Good value for the price important—didn't choose on appearance alone.

4. Answers will vary. Possible related words: *electronic device, equipment, headphones, batteries.*

ACTIVITY 2

Answers will vary. Possible answers to the four-step prediction process:

1. The topic is probably a planned U.S. journey to explore the planet Mars. The word "mission" probably means a journey, exploration, or scientific research.

2. Possible brainstormed responses:

- The plans have been announced, so the article may tell us when the mission will take place and what will be done on the mission.
- It might involve some kind of scientific research. Will astronauts try to walk on Mars, or just send equipment there?

3. Possible notes (facts or memories recalled about the topic):
   - There have been news reports over the past few years about scientific tests done on Mars.
   - The U.S. has sent robots to Mars but not people.
   - They are not sure if there is water on Mars or if that planet could support life.
   - Is it very cold on Mars—or very hot?

4. Possible related words: *astronaut, outer space, atmosphere, terrain, extraterrestrial.*

Asking Questions About the Text
Student Book p. 13

Understanding the Strategy
Possible additional wh- question words or phrases: *how much, whose, which, how long.*

ACTIVITY 3

Answers may vary. Possible questions:

A. How did Wangari Maathai first become interested in planting seeds?
   Where is Kenya?
   What kind of trees did Wangari Maathai plant?
   Which direction has her interest gone in? (Formal English: In which direction has her interest gone?)
   What else has Wangari Maathai done to help the environment?

B. Why is NASA using a new telescope?
   What will NASA see with the new telescope?
   Who will use the new telescope? (Who uses the Hubble Telescope now?)
   How long has the Hubble Telescope been in use?

C. What is a "first lady"?
   What causes child poverty?
   How can people fight child poverty?
   How long did the conference last?

Read

Marking the Text
Student Book p. 15

ACTIVITY 4

Answers may vary. Possible ways of marking the text:

- Exclamation point at the end of paragraph 1: students may be surprised to learn that an adult may just walk away from a learning situation!
- In paragraph 2, list the benefits of classroom practice: 1. Students can practice the language. 2. Many people learn better socially. 3. Students more likely to continue if they feel they're part of a group.
- Possible important new words to circle: *enthusiastic, motivated, knowledgeable, sensitive, creative.*
- Put a note after the last statement: Some students learn well and will continue regardless of the social environment because they are determined to succeed.

Reading More than Once
Student Book p. 16

ACTIVITY 5

Self-assessment questions; answers will vary.

Using Connectors to Follow Ideas
Student Book p. 17

ACTIVITY 6

1. We = Dave and I
2. He = a young black horse
3. she = a strong white mare
4. They = the young black horse and the strong white mare (the two horses)
5. it = the field
6. It = no referent ("empty it"; statement about the weather)
7. we = Dave and I

CHAPTER 1   3

ACTIVITY 7

1. He = Sam; she = "Rosie," his car
2. He = my dog
3. They = many people in my school
4. It = no referent ("empty it")
5. he = Jack; we = Jack and I
6. it = no referent ("empty it"; question about time)
7. they = Marge and Mike; her = Carol
8. it = no referent ("empty it"; statement about the weather); they = farmers

Using Signal Words to Predict Ideas
Student Book p. 19

ACTIVITY 8

Sentence completions will vary. Answers to questions:

1. This person is likely not going to help you; the signal word *but* indicates contrast.
2. A reason for Jenny's not going to the party will come next; *since* introduces a reason or cause.
3. The teacher probably returned the tests. *Finally* indicates a conclusion, or the final step in a process, sometimes after much delay.

ACTIVITY 9

1. c. people are too busy to pay attention. (signal word = *but*, indicating contrast)
2. c. there is so much to do, we must work together. (signal word = *because*, indicating cause or reason)

3. b. work hard. (signal word = *and*, indicating additional information)
4. a. the job will be quite difficult. (signal word = *Consequently*, indicating conclusion or result)
5. a. we have already saved many animals. (signal word = *For example*, indicating an example)

ACTIVITY 10

Answers will vary. Possible predictions:

1. it snows a lot / it's expensive to heat homes / it's hard to get around in the snow and ice
2. it may not win this year / many people would rather see Italy win / the U.S. team may have a chance this year
3. your injury has not completely healed / you're not feeling well / the gym is closed today
4. Indian curries use a lot of strong spices / Malaysian dishes use certain beans and fruits that are not commonly used in other styles of cooking / sushi can have many different flavors
5. we found her / she appeared / we gave up
6. wrote novels / illustrated them / enjoyed reading stories written by other people

Remember

Using Pictures
Student Book p. 21

ACTIVITY 11

Answers will vary.

PART 2 · VOCABULARY STRATEGIES

Deciding Which Words Are Important
Student Book p. 22

ACTIVITY 12

The word that is key to the main idea is *migratory*. The word is repeated in the passage. The word probably means to travel or to move from one place to another.

Looking for Internal Definitions
Student Book p. 23

ACTIVITY 13

1. Before each flight, (the crew chief), the mechanic who works on the plane, inspects the plane. Signal = . . . , . . . (comma before the internal definition).

2. The pilot then makes his ("walk around")—the inspection of the outside of the plane. Signal = —(a long dash before the internal definition).

3. He received a thousand (gold reales), gold coins, for his work. Signal = , ... , (commas before and after the internal definition).

4. The (gauges), or dials, are not correct. Signal = or.

5. The teacher told him that his paper was (faultless), in other words, perfect. Signal = in other words.

6. For the first two years I was a (peripatetic) teacher. That is, I went to many schools so that I could teach in many types of classrooms. Signal = That is.

7. (Meteorology), the study of the weather, is very interesting. Signal = , ... , (commas before and after the internal definition).

8. The company is doing a (pilot) or test of their new medicine. Signal = or.

9. Your home, your town, the countryside around you is (your environment). No signal. The sentence clearly states the definition using the verb is.

Using Synonyms, Antonyms, and Restatements
Student Book p. 24

ACTIVITY 14

Guesses of word meanings may vary. Possible answers:

1. *Massive* probably means very big. (synonym: *largest*)
2. *Herpetology* probably means the study of something. (synonym: *the study of snakes*)
3. *Knapsack* probably means a bag in which you put things. (synonym: *backpacks*)
4. To be *in big trouble* probably means to have a big problem, or to have done something wrong. (restatement: *In other words, she said he was going to flunk the class.*)

ACTIVITY 15

Guesses of word meanings may vary. Possible answers:

1. *Blithely* probably means happily, or without concern or worry. (antonym: *unhappy*)
2. *Imbecile* probably means stupid or not smart. (antonym: *smartest*)
3. *Arches* probably means a kind of structure shaped like a half circle, or with a curve. (antonym: *straight lines*)
4. *Insignificant* probably means not important. (antonym: *very important*)

ACTIVITY 16

Guesses of word meanings may vary. Possible answers:

1. *Kachina* probably means a kind of toy or a doll; it might be an Indian name. (synonym: *Hopi Indian dolls*)
2. *Plankton* probably means a type of food found in the sea, a kind of fish. (restatement: *The main food of most whales*)
3. *Emancipation* probably means freedom or liberation from something. (synonym: *freedom*)
4. *Ultimately* probably means in the end, or finally; the end result of something. (antonym: *at first*)
5. *Migrate* probably means to travel or to move from one place to another. (antonym: *stay*)
6. *The enormity of the predicament* probably means the big size of a problem. (restatement: *the size of the problem*)
7. *Populous* probably means having a lot of people; populated. (antonym: *the smallest number of people*)
8. *Capacious* probably means large or with a lot of space, maybe having many rooms. (antonym: *cramped*)
9. *Mimicry* probably means resembling other animals, looking like (mimicking, imitating) something else. (restatement: *Many defenseless animals look like poisonous or dangerous ones.*)
10. *Hibernation* probably means sleeping for a long time, especially during the winter; it may be something that only animals do. (restatement: *sleep through most of the winter*)
11. *Inflation* probably means an increase in prices. (restatement: *prices of goods rose unbelievably high*)
12. *Plummeted* probably means dropped suddenly,

or dropped very low; decreased, lowered. (restatement: *fallen so quickly*)

13. *Graze* probably means to eat vegetation or grass (something that animals do, how some animals eat). (restatement: the *animals eat the plants*)

14. *Devices* probably means tools, instruments, or special features. (synonym: *instruments*)

15. *Hawaii* is probably a place that is very beautiful, almost like a paradise. (restatement: *paradise on earth*)

Reading: Fire!

Getting Started
Student Book p. 27

Answers will vary. Possible answers:

1. The chapter is about fire. It might also be about different types of fires, what happens during a fire, or how to put out certain kinds of fires.
2. Answers will vary.
3. A fire can be put out with water (buckets or hoses), a fire extinguisher, or dirt/sand thrown on top of the fire.

Prepare
Student Book p. 28

1. b. things necessary for fire (The title includes the word "elements.")
2. Possible words connected to *fire*: *oxygen, fuel, smoke, flame, heat, temperature, burn, extinguish, put out.*
3. Pre-reading question will vary. Possible questions:
   - What does a fire need to burn?
   - How can a fire start?
   - How can a fire be put out?

Read
Student Book p. 28

Answers to the possible prediction questions from the *Prepare* section:

- Fires need oxygen, fuel, and heat.
- Fires can start when oxygen, fuel, and heat are all present, and there is enough heat to burn the type of fuel that is available.
- A fire can be put out by taking away or reducing one of the three ingredients (take away the oxygen, heat, or fuel).

Read Again
Student Book p. 29

Practice of individual reading strategies should be encouraged; answers will vary.

Possible additional questions and answers:

Question: What are some different types of fuels?

Answer: Paper and wood are fuels.

Question: What if one of the things fire needs to burn is missing?

Answer: If one thing is missing, the fire won't burn.

For connectors (pronouns) and referents, see *C. Following Ideas* on TM page 7.

Signal words and predictions:

- *And* (lines 1, 2, 4, 5, 7, 14, 17) indicates additional information.
- *For example* (line 2) indicates an example.
- *Because* (lines 2, 3) indicates a reason.
- *However* (line 2) indicates contrasting information.

- *Also* (lines 6, 10) indicates additional information.
- *Another* (line 12) indicates additional information.

Post-Reading Activities

A. Comprehension Check

1. F 2. T 3. F 4. N 5. N 6. T

B. Vocabulary Check

1. **a.** put out **b.** go out, take away **c.** use up
2. Answers for some categories, such as "Can I guess or should I look in a dictionary?" will vary. Some sections of the chart may be completed as follows:

Word	Is it important?	Is there an internal definition?	Is there an illustration?	Meaning
1. oxygen	Yes (The word repeats, and it is in the diagram.)	Yes (line 1)	No, but it is part of an illustration; it is a "side" of fire in the diagram.	Oxygen is a common gas. It has no color, taste, or smell, and it is found in our atmosphere (air) and in water. It can combine with other elements.
2. fuel	Yes (The word repeats, and it is in the diagram.)	Yes (lines 1–2)	No, but it is part of an illustration; it is a "side" of fire in the diagram.	Any burnable material.
3. amount	Yes (The word is used only once, but there are other words—reduce, lower—that refer to the amount of heat.)	No	No	The quantity, degree, or number of something.
4. triangle	Yes (The word repeats, and it is in the diagram.)	Yes (lines 5–7)	Yes (the fire triangle diagram)	A shape with three sides.
5. reduce	Yes (The word is only used once, but there is a synonym, *lower*.)	Yes (line 9) Synonym: *lower*	No	To lower, or to lessen the amount of.
6. material	Yes (The word repeats.)	Yes (line 2) Examples: *paper*, *wood*	No	A material is any physical matter; it can be seen or touched, perceived through the senses. Materials are also things of which something is made, things that are worked into a more finished form.

CHAPTER 2   7

C. Following Ideas

1. they = paper and wood
   it = water
2. They = firefighters
   They = firefighters
   they = firefighters

Remember
Student Book p. 31

Answers will vary. Students may draw a diagram of the fire triangle from memory.

Discuss
Student Book p. 31

1. Answers will vary. Possible answer: Materials that burn easily include paper, wood, fabrics, grease, gasoline, and plastic. Fires can be put out with water, fire extinguishers, or taking away the oxygen (if the fire is small).
2. Answer will vary. Possible answer: Materials that do not burn include brick, rock, stone, ceramic/clay, metal, and glass. Products that use these materials include the exteriors of some houses, fireplaces (brick), and file cabinets.

Prepare
Student Book p. 31

1. b. how to fight wildfires
2. Possible words connected to *wildfires*: burn, spread, haze, forests, spread.
3. Pre-reading questions will vary. Possible questions:
   • How do wildfires start?
   • How can wildfires be controlled?

Read
Student Book p. 31

Answers to the possible prediction questions from the *Prepare* section:
   • Wildfires can start because of lightning, accidents, and arson.
   • Wildfires can be controlled with controlled burns, which use fire to put out fire (or to prevent wildfires from spreading).

Read Again
Student Book p. 32

Practice of individual reading strategies should be encouraged; answers will vary.

Possible additional questions and answers:
   Question: What is a controlled burn?
   Answer: A controlled burn is a fire that firefighters start and control themselves.
   Question: How do firefighters use controlled burns?
   Answer: Firefighters use them to make firebreaks, an area that a wildfire cannot cross.
   Question: What is a firebreak?
   Answer: An area of ground with no fuel.

For connectors (pronouns) and referents, see *C. Following Ideas* on TM page 9.

Signal words and predictions:
   • *And* (lines 2, 3, 5, 8, 17, 20, 27, 29) indicates additional information.
   • *Also* (line 10) indicates additional information.
   • *For example* (lines 12–13, 25) indicates an example.
   • *In 2001* (line 13) indicates time or chronology of events.
   • *Because* (line 15) indicates a reason.
   • *Are examples of* (line 20) indicates an example.
   • *However* (line 30) indicates contrasting information.

Post-Reading Activities

A. Comprehension Check

1. Lightning is a natural event that may cause a wildfire.
2. People can start wildfires accidentally by being careless with campfires or matches or purposely (arson).
3. A controlled burn helps to control a wildfire by destroying the fuel for a fire. It uses up the

available fuel, and it creates a "firebreak," an area of ground that has no fuel. Fire then cannot spread across the firebreak.

4. Controlled burns can be small fires, but they can also be very large, even the size of a small town.

5. Weather is important for a controlled burn because wind can spread a fire.

6. Firefighters do use controlled burns near homes to prevent wildfires from spreading and destroying property. However, they do not use controlled burns near homes if the weather is bad.

B. Vocabulary Check

1. An arsonist is a person who purposely starts a fire.

2. Other compound words with "fire":

   wildfire = a fire that occurs in the wilderness, in a forest

   campfire = a controlled fire that is created in a campsite for warmth or for cooking

   firebreak = an area of ground that has no fuel for a fire

3. Answers for some categories, such as "Can I guess or should I look in a dictionary?" will vary. Some sections of the chart may be completed as follows:

Word	Is it important?	Is there an internal definition?	Is there an illustration?	Meaning
1. destroy	Yes (The word repeats.)	No	No	Ruin or greatly damage.
2. acres	Yes (The word repeats.)	No	No	Units of measurement for land, usually farmland or wilderness. An acre is equal to approximately 43,560 square feet, or 4,047 square meters.
3. forests	Yes (It is found in the sentence 1 of paragraph 1, a main idea.)	No	No	Areas of land that are covered with trees; woods; wilderness.
4. lightning	Yes (The word repeats and is used in paragraph 1 as a main cause of wildfires.)	Partially (line 2) We learn where lightning comes from and that it can start fires.	No	A big spark of electricity that can be produced during a thunderstorm.

CHAPTER 2   9

Word	Is it important?	Is there an internal definition?	Is there an illustration?	Meaning
5. crime	Yes (It is used in the definition of another key word, *arson*.)	Partially (line 3) We learn that *arson is a type of crime*, but no precise definition.	No	An illegal activity, something that goes against the law.
6. controlled burn	Yes (The word repeats.)	Yes (lines 8–11)	No	A fire that firefighters start and control themselves.
7. varies	Yes	Partially (lines 9–11) The word is not defined, but examples are given that help explain the word.	No	Changes, differs, or reflects a variety (or range) of options.

Choices of additional unfamiliar words will vary. Possible unfamiliar, important words: *property, natural, effective, spread*.

C. Following Ideas

They = firefighters

it = a controlled burn

It = a controlled burn

they = firefighters

them = controlled burns

it = no referent ("empty it," describing the weather)

Remember
Student Book p. 34

Answers will vary. Students may draw a map of a forest with a river to show a natural firebreak; they may also draw an area where a controlled burn creates a firebreak and stops a fire.

Discuss
Student Book p. 34

Answers will vary.

Prepare
Student Book p. 34

1. The reading is about a famous fire in history: the Great Chicago Fire.

2. Possible words connected to *famous city fires*: *firefighters, destroy, flames, buildings, streets, sidewalks*.

3. Pre-reading questions will vary. Possible questions:
   • How did the Great Chicago Fire start?
   • How long did the Great Chicago Fire burn?

Read
Student Book p. 34

Answers to the possible prediction questions from the *Prepare* section:

- No one is sure how the fire started, but it may have begun in a barn, and the conditions were good for a fire: trees were dry, and the wind was strong.
- The fire burned for almost three days.

Read Again
Student Book p. 35

Practice of individual reading strategies should be encouraged; answers will vary.

Possible additional questions and answers:

  Question: Why is the fire called "great"?

  Answer: Because it was a very large fire.

  Question: How much of Chicago did the fire destroy?

  Answer: It destroyed most of the city, an area four miles long and three quarters of a mile wide.

For connectors (pronouns) and referents, see *C. Following Ideas* on TM page 11.

Signal words and predictions:

- *And* (lines 3, 5, 6, 9, 19, 22, 24, 25, 27) indicates additional information.
- *Around* (line 10) indicates time or chronology of events.
- *By* (lines 11, 16) indicates time or chronology of events.
- *Also* (line 15) indicates additional information.
- *Finally* (line 18) indicates conclusion.
- *However* (line 19) indicates contrasting information.
- *By that time* (lines 19–20) indicates time or chronology of events.
- *In the end* (line 21) indicates conclusion.
- *But* (line 30) indicates contrasting information.
- *18 months later* (lines 31–32) indicates time or chronology of events.

Post-Reading Activities

A. Comprehension Check

1. It is not known who started the fire. It may have started in a barn.
2. The fire spread quickly because the trees were dry, the wind was strong, and there was a lot of wood fuel (streets, sidewalks, boats, etc.).
3. Firefighters stopped fighting the fire at 3:30 A.M. when the water pumping station burned down. Without water, they could not fight the fire.
4. The fire burned for approximately three days.
5. Rain finally put the fire out.
6. The burned area was four miles long and three quarters of a mile wide—more than 2,000 acres.
7. It took Chicagoans just 18 months to rebuild their city.

B. Vocabulary Check

1. Two phrases that mean "started to burn": *burst into flames, caught fire*.
2. Answers for some categories, such as "Can I guess or should I look in a dictionary?" will vary. Some sections of the chart may be completed as follows:

Word	Is it important?	Is there an internal definition?	Is there an illustration?	Meaning
1. headed	No	No	No	Traveled, went in a particular direction.
2. water pumping station	Yes	No	No	A building where firefighters have access to water for fighting fires.

Word	Is it important?	Is there an internal definition?	Is there an illustration?	Meaning
3. fireproof	Yes (The use of quotation marks around the word calls special attention to it.)	No	No	Resistant to fire; not able to burn.
4. died out	Yes	No	No	Ended; stopped burning.
5. in ruins	Yes	Yes (lines 21, 26) Similar words: *destroyed, lost*	No	Destroyed, wrecked.
6. rebuilding	Yes	Yes (lines 20, 21) Contrasting words: *in ruins, destroyed*	No	Building again.
7. celebration	Yes	No	No	Festival, happy event, party.
8. rebirth	Yes	No	No	New beginning.

Choices of additional unfamiliar words will vary. Possible unfamiliar, important words: *barn, acres, honor/in honor of*.

C. Following Ideas

1. that time = Tuesday morning
   This area = the area (destroyed by the fire) four miles long, and three quarters of a mile wide—more than 2,000 acres
2. It (line 3) = no referent ("empty *it*", statement about days)
   it (line 8) = the fire
   it (line 8) = the fire

D. Predicting Ideas with Signal Words

1. a. around = line 10
   b. by = lines 11, 16
   c. by that time = lines 19–20
   d. finally = lines 18, 19
   e. in the end = line 21

2. Each signal word listed introduces a time; each signal word predicts steps in a process or sequence (time organization).

3. a. around = connects where the fire was when it started to where it traveled to around midnight
   b. by = in line 12, connects what happened around midnight to what had happened by 3:30 A.M.
   = in line 16, connects what had happened by 3:30 A.M. to what had happened by noon on Monday
   c. by that time = connects what happened on Tuesday morning to what happened by (or before) that time, the fact that the city was in ruins
   d. finally = connects the two events on Tuesday morning—the rain began to fall and the flames died out
   e. in the end = connects all the events of the fire with the final results, the extent of the destruction in the city

12 CHAPTER 2

Remember
Student Book p. 37

Illustrations will vary. Maps should include a downtown section and a river, and show a movement from south to north.

Discuss
Student Book p. 37

Answers will vary. Possible answers:

1. The fire spread so quickly because conditions for fire were good. The trees were dry (it was autumn), and there was a strong wind to carry the fire. The river had oil and wooden boats, and the sidewalks and streets were wooden, which could serve as fuel for the fire.

2. A fire this big might be less likely in a city today because cities today do not use so much wood. In the past, cities had wooden sidewalks and many wooden buildings. Additionally, today there are more firefighters, more fire stations, and there is easier access to water to fight fires (fire hydrants). Buildings have more fireproof materials than they used to. However, fires are still possible and can spread quickly.

Prepare
Student Book p. 37

Answers may vary. Possible answers:

1. Coal fires are fires that burn in coalmines underground. Reading the title and skimming the article are strategies that can help determine the topic.

2. Possible words connected to *coal* and *fires*: mines, pollution, natural, burn, control.

3. Pre-reading questions will vary. Possible questions:
   - What causes coal fires?
   - How can coal fires be put out?

Read
Student Book p. 38

Answers to the possible prediction questions from the *Prepare* section:

- Coal fires can start from natural causes or when people burn garbage in old mines.
- Coal fires are hard to put out; they can be put out when they are still small, but when they are too big, they are impossible to put out and can burn for years.

Read Again
Student Book p. 38

Practice of individual reading strategies should be encouraged; answers will vary.

Possible additional questions and answers:

Question: Why do the underground fires keep burning?

Answer: Because they have fuel, oxygen, and heat.

Question: How long do coal fires burn for?

Answer: They can burn for many years.

For connectors (pronouns) and referents, see *C. Following Ideas* on TM page 13.

Signal words and predictions:

- *But* (line 4) indicates contrasting information.
- *Because* (lines 4, 10) indicates a reason.
- *Such as* (lines 8–9, 28) indicates an example.
- *Also* (line 9) indicates additional information.
- *And* (lines 11, 13, 17, 20, 26, 29) indicates additional information.
- *About 2,000 years ago* (line 19) indicates time or chronology of events.
- *In 1916* (line 20) indicates time or chronology of events.
- *For 20 years* (lines 22–23) indicates time or chronology of events.
- *In 1983* (line 23) indicates time or chronology of events.
- *Finally* (line 23) indicates a conclusion.
- *In one year* (line 24) indicates time or chronology of events.

Post-Reading Activities

A. Comprehension Check

1. The fire in Colorado started more than 50 years ago, and no one has ever seen it because it burns 65 feet underground.

2. Satellites will help scientists fight these fires (by detecting fires when they are still small).
3. These fires can start from natural causes, like lightning, or from people burning garbage in old mines.
4. These fires are difficult to control because there is so much fuel, oxygen, and heat underground.
5. These fires cause air pollution and may cause residents of a whole town to move.

B. Vocabulary Check

1. The words that are not important to the main idea of this sentence are *Institute, Aerospace,* and *Survey*. It is only important to understand that someone is studying the problem. The word *geologist* might be important to know because it states what he/she does (a *geologist* studies earth sciences).

2. Answers for some categories, such as "Can I guess or should I look in a dictionary?" will vary. Some sections of the chart may be completed as follows:

Word	Is it important?	Is there an internal definition?	Meaning
1. huge	No (It is a description word.)	Possibly (line 16) Similar word: *too big*	Very big.
2. underground	Yes (The word repeats.)	Yes (line 6) Opposite idea: *above the earth*	Below the earth.
3. satellites	Yes (The word appears in a topic sentence.)	No	An object that orbits the earth in space and can take pictures of, or detect, certain features in the earth.
4. garbage	Yes (It is mentioned as a cause of these fires.)	No	Trash, waste, refuse.
5. geologist	Yes	No	A type of scientist who studies the earth/earth sciences.
6. residents	Yes	Yes (lines 21-22) Examples: *people of Centralia, Pennsylvania*	People who live in a place or community.

Choices of additional unfamiliar words will vary. Possible unfamiliar, important words: *experts, pollution*.

C. Following Ideas

1. it = this fire
   it's = this fire
2. They = these fires/underground coal fires
3. He = Anupma Prakash
   it = no referent (pronoun subject)
   they = the fires
4. they = coal fires
5. they = the people of Centralia, Pennsylvania

14 CHAPTER 2

Remember
Student Book p. 40

The chart may be completed as follows:

Fire	Cause(s)	Time Fire Lasts/Lasted	Kinds of Damage	How Put Out
1. underground coal fires	natural causes (like lightning) and garbage burning in old coalmines	can last for years, even as long as 2,000 years	air pollution	unclear from the reading; possibly remove some of the fire's fuel
2. wildfires	lightning, accidents, and arson	can last for days or weeks	destruction of property (forestland and private property, nearby homes); lives lost	water, and also the use of controlled burns—fighting fire with fire
3. Great Chicago Fire	unknown; possibly dry conditions and wind	approximately three days	acres of property destroyed, lives lost	rain

Discuss
Student Book p. 40

1. Students can be encouraged to review and discuss their charts or the notes they made in preparation for filling out the chart.
2. Answers will vary. Possible answers: Underground coal fires ARE as dangerous as other fires because they cause air pollution, which is dangerous to people's health and might even kill people over time. **(OR)** Underground coal fires ARE NOT as dangerous as other fires because they do not cause visible destruction of land or property, they do not endanger people's lives, and they burn in a contained environment—they do not spread.

Reading: The Extraordinary Shark

Getting Started
Student Book p. 42

Answers will vary. Possible answer to #1:

1. This chapter will probably talk about why sharks are very interesting or amazing animals. It might talk about different kinds of sharks, where sharks live, and what sharks eat.

Prepare
Student Book p. 43

Answers may vary. Possible answers:

1. a. key facts about sharks
2. Possible terms that might be in the text: *teeth, attack, fins, dangerous, kill, hunt.*

3. Pre-reading questions will vary. Possible questions:
   - What do sharks eat?
   - Are sharks dangerous?

Read
Student Book p. 43

Answers to the possible prediction questions from the *Prepare* section:
- Sharks eat meat. They eat dolphins, seals, other sharks, and other fish.
- Sharks can be dangerous—they are good hunters, and they kill with their sharp teeth. However, they are also interesting animals and good survivors.

Read Again
Student Book p. 44

Practice of individual reading strategies should be encouraged; answers will vary.

Possible additional questions and answers:

Question: Why are sharks successful?

Answer: Because they are such good hunters.

Question: How many kinds of sharks exist?

Answer: There are more than 350 different kinds of sharks.

For connectors (pronouns) and referents, see *C. Following Ideas* on TM page 17.

Signal words and predictions:
- *Also* (lines 1, 6, 19, 27) indicates additional information.
- *However* (lines 1, 8) indicates contrasting information.
- *But* (lines 4, 17) indicates contrasting information.
- *First of all* (line 4) indicates time or chronology of events.
- *And* (lines 5, 18) indicates additional information.
- *In fact* (line 9) indicates emphasis.
- *In addition* (line 10) indicates additional information.
- *Consequently* (line 12) indicates an effect or result.
- *For example* (line 18) indicates an example.
- *Another* (line 22) indicates additional information.
- *After* (line 24) indicates time or chronology of events.

Post-Reading Activities

A. Comprehension Check

1. Sharks came before dinosaurs.
2. There are more than 350 different kinds of sharks.
3. Sharks become adults when they are between 10 and 15 years old.
4. Shark bones do not break easily because they are tough and flexible.
5. Sharks use their teeth for killing, not for chewing.
6. Shark families do not always live together. Young sharks may stay close to the shore to grow up alone. A shark may leave her babies after giving birth.

B. Vocabulary Check

1. A shark's body has gill slits, or openings that help the shark breathe in the water. Its bones are tough and flexible. A shark's skin has sharp spikes or nails. Shark bones are compared to a human ear because both are tough and flexible at the same time.

2. Answers for some categories, such as "Can I guess or should I look in a dictionary?" will vary. Some sections of the chart may be completed as follows:

Word	Is it important?	Is there an internal definition?	Is there an illustration?	Meaning
1. species	Yes (The word appears in the introduction and a topic sentence, and the word repeats.)	Yes (line 15) *There are more than 350 different kinds of sharks.*	No	Kind, type, group, category of living things.
2. carnivore	Yes (The word is defined.)	Yes (line 5)	No	Meat eater.
3. cold-blooded	Yes (The word is defined.)	Yes (line 6)	No	Having a body temperature that changes as the water temperature changes.
4. gill slits	Yes (The word is defined.)	Yes (lines 7–8)	Yes	Openings that help the shark breathe in the water.
5. armor	Yes	Yes (lines 11–12)	Yes	It has many sharp spikes or nails to protect it.
6. spikes	Yes	No	Yes	Sharp, pointy things; often used for self-defense or self-protection.
7. survive	Yes (The word repeats in a different form.)	Yes (lines 16–17)	No	Live on.
8. hunter	Yes (Examples of how they are great hunters are given.)	Yes (lines 18–19)	No	Something that finds and kills its own food.
9. chew	Yes	Yes (lines 20–21) Opposite idea: *They swallow their food whole or in big pieces.*	No	Use the teeth to break food into small pieces before swallowing.

Word	Is it important?	Is there an internal definition?	Is there an illustration?	Meaning
10. swallow	No	No	No	Ingest/eat food or liquid (either without chewing, or after chewing).
11. pups	Yes (The word repeats.)	Yes (lines 22–23) Synonyms: *young, babies*	No	Young, babies, offspring.
12. litter	No	Yes (lines 22–23)	No	Many pups produced at one time.
13. survivors	Yes (The word repeats in a different form.)	Yes (lines 16–17)	No	Things that live on.

Choices of additional unfamiliar words will vary. Possible unfamiliar, important words: *species, dolphins, seals, skeleton.*

C. Following Ideas

Pronoun	Line	Refers to
1. they	5	sharks
2. it	11	a shark
3. they	15	sharks
4. they	24	shark pups

D. Predicting Ideas with Signal Words

1. a. also = lines 1, 6, 19, 27
   b. consequently = line 12
   c. first of all = line 4
   d. however = lines 1, 8
   e. in addition = line 10
   f. in fact = line 9

2. a. also = connects two fish-like characteristics of sharks: they are cold-blooded and they have gill slits. The signal word predicts additional information.

   b. consequently = connects a characteristic of the shark's armor-like skin (*it has many sharp spikes or nails*) with what can happen if you touch it (*you can hurt yourself*). The signal word predicts a result.

   c. first of all = connects the idea that sharks and fish have some things in common but are also different with the example that sharks, unlike fish, are meat eaters. The signal word predicts the first item or example in a sequence.

   d. however = connects the fact that everyone knows what sharks look like and that they are dangerous with the idea that not everyone realizes that sharks are an old species and interesting. The signal word predicts contrasting information.

   e. in addition = connects the two characteristics of a shark's bones with a characteristic of a shark's skin. The signal word predicts additional information.

   f. in fact = connects two characteristics of a shark's bones: they are tough and flexible, and they feel like a human ear. The signal word predicts additional information, with emphasis.

18 CHAPTER 3

3. Answers may vary. Possible answers: *Consequently* could also predict other results or effects of a shark's sharp, armor-like skin. For example, it could predict how other animals are affected when they touch it, or how the skin might protect the shark during an attack by another shark or another animal.
In addition could also predict another type of difference between a shark and a fish. For example, it could introduce a fact about its eyesight or its hearing.

Remember
Student Book p. 46

Illustrations will vary. The following parts should be included and labeled: gill slits, spikes on the skin. Students may include a skeleton as well; some students may also draw a fin on the top.

Discuss
Student Book p. 46

Answers will vary. Possible answers:

1. Sharks are more dangerous because they are very good hunters, they eat many different kinds of fish and animals, and they have many sharp teeth that they use only for killing. Whales may be dangerous because of their size, but they do not seem to hunt and attack in the way that sharks do.
2. Dinosaurs may have died out because they lacked necessary skills to survive or to defend themselves against certain kinds of attacks or threats. Sharks, however, are very good at protecting themselves and surviving.

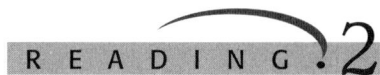

Prepare
Student Book p. 47

Answers will vary. Possible answers:

1. The topic of the reading is the senses of sharks: how sharks use their senses and how sharks' jaws work. The strategies of predicting from the title and headings, and skimming for the definitions of the key words (boldfaced) can be used.
2. In hunting, good eyesight is very important. Smell and hearing might also be important. Speed and strength are important.
3. Pre-reading questions will vary. Possible questions:
   • How well can a shark see?
   • What can a shark smell?

Read
Student Book p. 47

Answers to the possible prediction questions from the *Prepare* section:

• A shark can see very well, even when there is little light. However, a shark can't see what is directly in front of him without moving his head from side to side.
• A shark can smell blood.

Read Again
Student Book p. 47

Practice of individual reading strategies should be encouraged; answers will vary.

Possible additional questions and answers:

Question: How well can sharks hear?
Answer: Sharks have very sensitive ears and can hear very well.

Question: What are sharks' jaws like?
Answer: Sharks' jaws are unique. They are made of cartilage, contain several rows of teeth, and are very powerful.

For connectors (pronouns) and referents, see *C. Following Ideas* on TM page 20.

CHAPTER 3   **19**

Post-Reading Activities

A. Comprehension Check

Answers may vary. The chart may be completed as follows:

Why Sharks are Great Hunters

Shark Characteristic	Example
Sharks have amazing sensory equipment that helps them find their prey.	Sharks can feel, see, smell, and hear extremely well.
Sharks can notice even small changes in their environment.	Sharks can sense weak electricity that small fish create when they breathe.
A shark's eyes are sensitive.	Sharks can see even when there is very little light.
Sharks have especially sensitive ears.	Sharks can hear sounds of 200 yards to 1/4 of a mile (182.88 to 402.336m) away.
Sharks are extremely powerful and can easily kill other animals.	A shark's jaws contain several rows of very sharp teeth. When a tooth is lost, it is replaced. A great white shark can bite with a pressure of 2,000 pounds per square inch (140.614 kg/sq cm).

B. Vocabulary Check

1. a. senses b. sensory c. sensitive d. sense
2. *Very* is the synonym for all the italicized words.
3. Answers for some categories, such as "Can I guess or should I look in a dictionary?" will vary. Some sections of the chart may be completed as follows:

Word	Is it important?	Is there an internal definition?	Meaning
1. equipment	Yes (The word appears in the introduction, and is mentioned as a reason for the main idea.)	No	Features, characteristics.
2. prey	Yes (The word appears in the introduction and in the first reason for the main idea.)	Yes (line 3)	Other animals that can be killed for food.
3. environment	Yes (The word appears in the introduction/main idea.)	No	Surroundings, area.

20 CHAPTER 3

Word	Is it important?	Is there an internal definition?	Meaning
4. weak	No (It is a description word.)	No	Slight, a small amount, faint.
5. jaws	Yes (The word is a subheading and the word repeats.)	Yes (lines 13–15)	The parts of the mouth with teeth, upper and lower, used for biting and chewing.
6. cartilage	Yes (The word appears in a topic sentence.)	Partially (line 13) Contrasting idea: Cartilage is not bone.	A tough but flexible substance used for skeletons and some external features in some animals.
7. sharp	Yes (It's a description word, but it describes an important aspect of the topic.)	No	Having a thin edge or a fine point, capable of cutting or piercing something.
8. pressure	Yes (A specific amount of pressure is given in the sentence; we need to know what "pressure" is in order to understand the number.)	No	The application of force to something else.

Choices of additional unfamiliar words will vary. Possible unfamiliar, important words: *notice, contain, replace, powerful.*

C. Following Ideas

The pronoun reference chart should be completed as follows:

Pronoun	Line	Refers to
1. they	5	sharks
2. it	7	a shark
3. it	8	a shark
4. they	13	a shark's jaws
5. they	15	a great white shark's jaws

Remember
Student Book p. 50

Illustrations may vary. Illustrations should include jaws with several rows of sharp teeth. In addition, the eyes, nose (or nostrils), and ears, with the corresponding senses, may be labeled, and arrows included showing the distances of their hearing reaches.

Discuss
Student Book p. 50

Answers may vary. Possible answers:

1. Bats also have amazing senses. They do not see well, but they hear and smell extremely well. Dogs can hear sounds that humans cannot hear. Whales can hear and communicate sounds that humans cannot ordinarily hear.
2. Not many animals prey on sharks. Whales are bigger than sharks, and may eat them. However, humans sometimes prey on sharks.

Prepare

Student Book p. 50

Answers may vary. Possible answers:

1. The topic of the reading is shark attacks on humans.
2. Possible reasons why sharks attack people: Sharks may attack people because of hunger or anger. A shark may feel that a person swimming or surfing in the water is in the shark's territory. The shark may feel threatened and attack for self-protection. Possible terms related to this topic: *kill, attack, scare, frighten, threaten, injure.*
3. Myths are stories that are not true. Possible myths about sharks might be that sharks always attack and try to kill humans, or that all sharks are dangerous to humans.

Read Part A

Student Book p. 50

Possible answers to the prediction question from the *Prepare* section:

- The myths about sharks are untrue stories about sharks. One myth is that sharks are very dangerous to people.

Read Again

Student Book p. 51

For Part A, practice of individual reading strategies should be encouraged; answers will vary. Possible additional questions and answers:

Question: How many people are actually killed by sharks each year?

Answer: Only about 100 people are killed by sharks each year.

Question: Is there any other animal that kills more people?

Answer: Dogs kill thousands of people each year.

For Part B, the items in the graph represent the following kinds of information:

a. Dark red bars represent the number of shark attacks in the U.S.
b. Pink bars represent the number of shark attacks in the world.
c. The horizontal line represents the year.
d. The vertical line represents the number of shark attacks.

Post-Reading Activities

A. Comprehension Check

1. Most sharks are not dangerous to people because they are too small to kill people and they live in very deep water where humans don't swim.
2. According to Dr. Gruber, dogs are the most dangerous to people.
3. Sharks kill about 100 people every year.
4. People kill up to 100 million sharks every year.
5. In 2001, (about) 53 Americans were attacked by sharks.
6. In 2001, approximately 71 non-Americans were attacked by sharks.
7. The year 2000 had the most shark attacks.

B. Vocabulary Check

Answers for some categories, such as "Can I guess or should I look in a dictionary?" will vary. Some sections of the chart may be completed as follows:

Word	Is it important?	Is there an internal definition?	Is there an illustration?	Meaning
1. Rosenstiel	No (The word is part of the title of an institute, someone's name.)	No	No	No standard definition—name of a person.

Word	Is it important?	Is there an internal definition?	Is there an illustration?	Meaning
2. atmospheric	No (It is a description word and part of the title of an institute.)	No	No	Related to the environment.
3. expert	Yes (The word describes Dr. Gruber, who is described and quoted in the first paragraph, and the word repeats.)	No	No	Someone who has studied or knows a lot about something, someone with professional qualifications in a field.
4. myth	Yes (The word repeats, and is defined.)	Yes (line 3)	No	Untrue story.
5. trends	Yes (The word is used in the title of the graph.)	No	Yes (The bar graph shows trends, patterns, and changes over time.)	Patterns, developments, changes over time.
6. unprovoked	Yes (Although it is a description word, it is used in the title of the graph, so it's important.)	No	No	Done for no clear reason, with no apparent cause.

Choices of additional unfamiliar words will vary. Possible unfamiliar, important words: *biologist, marine, interview.*

C. Following Ideas

In the sentence, *it* has no referent (or antecedent). It is a subject pronoun.

D. Predicting Ideas with Signal Words

In Part A, the signal words predicting addition are as follows:

a. first = (line 4) connects the myth that sharks are dangerous with the first example of why this is a myth (*many sharks are too small to kill people*). The signal word predicts the first item or example in a series.

b. in addition = (line 5) connects the example that *many sharks are too small to kill people* with the example that *most sharks live in deep water, where people do not swim.* The signal word predicts a new or additional example.

c. also = (line 7) connects the example that elephants and dogs kill more people each year than sharks with the idea that *people are much more dangerous to sharks than sharks are to people.* The signal word predicts a new or additional example.

d. in fact = (line 8) connects the idea that *people are much more dangerous to sharks than sharks are to people* with the example that *people kill up to 100 million sharks each year.* The signal word predicts an additional example or point with an emphasis on truth.

CHAPTER 3   23

Remember
Student Book p. 52

Bar graphs may vary. Possible bar graph:

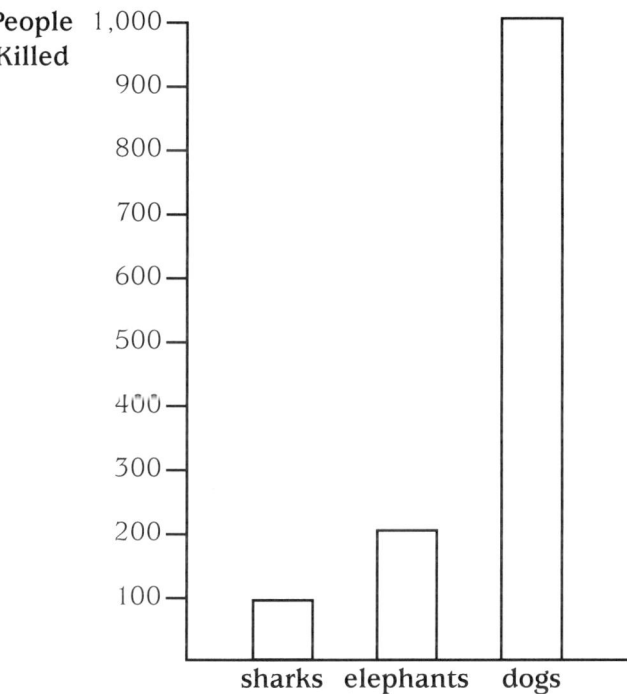

Discuss
Student Book p. 52

1. Answers will vary.
2. Answers may vary. Possible answer: "Fish Stories" is a casual title. It suggests that the article will just give information about fish. (OR) "Fish Stories" is a humorous title. "Stories" has a double meaning here; the article is talking about myths, or untrue stories, and "fish" is a light term for a shark. The reading is serious, however, explaining that some scientists believe sharks are not as dangerous as we think.

Prepare
Student Book p. 53

Answers may vary. Possible answers:

1. This reading is about a shark attack on a teenager. This can be determined by using the strategy of reading the title and skimming the article.
2. Possible terms related to shark attacks and injuries: *bite, bit, jaws, swimming, rescue, survive.*
3. Pre-reading questions will vary. Possible questions:
   * Why did the shark attack the teenager?
   * What happened to the teenager?
   * What happened to the shark?

Read
Student Book p. 53

Answers to the possible prediction questions from the *Prepare* section:

* The shark probably attacked the teenager because the teenager pulled his tail
* The teenager was bit in the chest and taken to the hospital. Doctors had to operate to remove the shark from his chest. The boy survived.
* The shark died.

Read Again
Student Book p. 53

Practice of individual reading strategies should be encouraged; answers will vary.

Possible additional questions and answers:

   Question: How large was the shark?
   Answer: He was very small—only three feet long.
   Question: What kind of shark was he?
   Answer: He was a nurse shark.

For connectors (pronouns) and referents, see *C. Following Ideas* on TM page 25.

Signal words and predictions:

* *After* (line 2) indicates time or chronology of events.
* *And* (lines 9, 11, 13, 16) indicates additional information.
* *Later* (line 13) indicates time or chronology of events.
* *However* (line 16) indicates contrasting information.

Post-Reading Activities

A. Comprehension Check

The events of the shark attack should be numbered as follows:

__1__ The boy was scuba diving.
__2__ The boy saw the shark.
__3__ The boy grabbed the shark's tail.
__4__ The shark bit the boy.
__5__ People took the boy and the shark to the hospital.
__6__ Doctors operated on the shark.
__7__ The shark died.
__8__ The doctors took care of the boy.
__9__ The boy went home.

B. Vocabulary Check

Answers for some categories, such as "Can I guess or should I look in a dictionary?" will vary. Some sections of the chart may be completed as follows:

Word	Is it important?	Is there an illustration?	Is there an internal definition?	Meaning
1. attached	Yes (The word appears in the first paragraph, in which the main idea is explained.)	No	Yes (line 3) *impossible to remove*	Connected, stuck onto.
2. chest	Yes (The word repeats, and it appears in the first paragraph and in a topic sentence.)	No	No	The area of the body above the stomach and below the neck
3. scuba diving	Yes (The word appears in a topic sentence, and it is the activity the boy was doing at the time of the attack.)	No	No	Diving deep below the surface of water, using an oxygen tank and other special equipment for air.
4. Marathon	No (The word is the name of a place.)	No	No	Name of a place in the Florida Keys.
5. operate	Yes (The word relates to the main idea of the story.)	No	No	Perform surgery.
6. harmless	Yes (The word appears in a topic sentence.)	No	Yes (line 17) Antonym: *dangerous*	Not capable of causing harm.

Choices of additional unfamiliar words will vary. Possible unfamiliar, important words: *sinks, remained, nurse shark, rescuers, patrol.*

CHAPTER 3   25

C. Following Ideas

The pronoun reference chart should be completed as follows:

Pronoun	Line	Refers to
1. it (was)	3	X (no referent)
2. its	9	the three-foot nurse shark
3. they	13	the doctors
4. they	16	nurse sharks

D. Predicting Ideas with Signal Words

1. The signal word *however* (line 16) predicts contrast.
2. The idea the signal word predicts is that nurse sharks can be dangerous.

   Possible restatement of the idea: Although nurse sharks seem harmless, they are dangerous and should be avoided. **(OR)** Nurse sharks seem safe, but they really aren't.

Remember
Student Book p. 55

This ordering of events is similar to *A. Comprehension Check*; however, students should scan the passage for the events themselves, number each new event, and illustrate it in their notebooks. They should then use their pictures to retell their stories without looking back at the text.

Discuss
Student Book p. 55

1. Answers will vary. Possible answer: The boy in the story did not act wisely. He should not have touched the shark. The shark probably got angry or felt afraid and was trying to protect itself.
2. Descriptions will vary. To extend this discussion activity, students could then write their descriptions.

Reading: All About Hair

Getting Started
Student Book p. 57

Answers will vary. Possible answers:

1. This hairstyle (a mohawk) was most popular in the late 1970s and early 1980s, especially in North America and in England. Some people who played or were interested in punk rock music had this hairstyle. Some people still have it today, though it isn't as popular.
2. Hair is important because it can by styled to express your identity and to attract people. In a society in which people are judged a lot on their appearance, hair is important. **(OR)** Hair is NOT important because you don't need it to survive; you can lose it and still function.

3. The readings might talk about different hairstyles throughout history, how hair grows, why people have different colors and textures of hair, or how to style your hair.

Prepare
Student Book p. 58

1. c. why hair is important
2. Possible opinions about hair: Some hairstyles are not appropriate for certain situations; people in the past wore their hair in ways that most of us would not wear it today; hairstyles today (or hairstyles for young people) are not attractive; men should wear their hair short

and women should wear their hair long; blondes have more fun; people with brown hair are more serious; women's hair can attract men and so it should be hidden under a scarf.

3. People have strong opinions about hair because it can express individual and cultural identity; people judge other people partly by the way they wear their hair. Hair is very important in some cultures, religions, and professions. Note: Students should also consider this pre-reading question as they read the article; additional possible answers are provided in the *Read* section below.

Read
Student Book p. 58

Possible answers to the question from the *Prepare* section:

- We think that changing our hair can change our lives. **(OR)** Hair can tell us about a person's attitude, work, religion, or ethnic origin.

Read Again
Student Book p. 59

Practice of individual reading strategies should be encouraged; answers will vary.

Students should underline the topic sentence (first sentence) of paragraphs 2 and 3. The examples in paragraph 2 illustrate the point that hair can be used as a form of social protest. The examples in paragraph 3 illustrate the point that hair can express religious and professional identity. Possible additional questions and answers:

Question: How can hair be used to show protest?

Answer: If society generally believes that people should wear their hair a certain way, wearing your hair differently shows protest.

Question: Why do soldiers around the world have short hair?

Answer: Maybe to show uniformity and conformity.

For connectors (pronouns) and referents, see *C. Following Ideas* on TM page 28.

Signal words and predictions:

- *And* (lines 4, 9, 16, 17, 19, 20) indicates additional information.
- *Because* (line 5) indicates a reason or a cause.
- *In the 1960s* (lines 7–8) indicates time or chronology of events.
- *At the same time* (lines 9–10) indicates time or chronology of events.
- *But* (line 14) indicates contrasting information.
- *For example* (lines 15, 19) indicates an example.

Post-Reading Activities

A. Comprehension Check

1. People try to change their hair by cutting it, curling it, straightening it, and dying it.
2. Many women tried to dye their hair blonde because a popular advertisement for hair dye once said "Blondes have more fun."
3. Examples of people using hairstyles for social protest include teenagers trying to look different from other people, African Americans growing Afros in the 1960s, and young men refusing to cut their hair in the 1960s.
4. Religious groups that can be identified by their hairstyles include Sikhs (from India), Hasidic Jews, and Rastafarians.
5. Lawyers and judges traditionally have conservative hairstyles (in England, they wear wigs in court); soldiers have short hair.

B. Vocabulary Check

1. **a.** curly, curl **b.** curls **c.** straighten **d.** straight
2. **a.** religion
3. Answers for some categories, such as "Can I guess or should I look in a dictionary?" will vary. Some sections of the chart may be completed as follows:

Word	Is it important?	Is there an internal definition?	Is there an illustration?	Meaning
1. dye	Yes (The word repeats.)	Yes (line 2)	No	Color/change the color.
2. protest	Yes (The word repeats, and it appears in topic sentences.)	No	No	Openly disagree with something; resist or refuse something.
3. bushy	Yes (The word is a description word, but here it's important because it defines a hairstyle that is important to the article.)	Yes (line 8) Contrasting information: *African Americans stopped straightening their hair.*	No	Very curly.
4. Afro	Yes (It has an internal definition.)	Yes (lines 8–9)	No	A hairstyle worn by African Americans in the 1960s; hair was allowed to grow long and bushy.
5. banned	Yes (It has an internal definition.)	Yes (lines 12–13) Restatement: *Only shorthaired men were allowed to visit.*	No	Forbidden, prohibited, prevented, did not allow (in this case, did not allow to visit).
6. identity	Yes (It appears in a topic sentence.)	No	No	Who you are, sense or image of oneself; personality or connections with certain groups.
7. peyes	Yes (It has an internal definition.)	Yes (line 17)	No	Long side curls, worn by Hasidic Jews.
8. dreadlocks	Yes (It has an internal definition.)	Yes (line 18)	No	Long braids.

28 CHAPTER 4

Word	Is it important?	Is there an internal definition?	Is there an illustration?	Meaning
9. turban	No	No	Yes	A cloth headpiece that wraps around the head or the hair, covering the hair.
10. wig	Yes (The word appears as an example of an important idea.)	No	Yes	An artificial hairpiece that can be removed; it can be made of real or synthetic hair, and may be in a certain style.

Choices of additional unfamiliar words will vary. Possible unfamiliar, important words: *improve, conservative, twist, court, attitude, ethnic origin.*

C. Following Ideas

The pronoun reference chart should be completed as follows:

Pronoun	Line	Refers to
1. it	2	hair (our hair)
2. it	4	the popular advertisement that "blondes have more fun"
3. it	5	hair
4. they	9	African Americans

Remember
Student Book p. 61

Illustrations will vary. Students may draw and label pictures of long hair, short hair, straight hair, and curly hair. They may draw a teenager with different hair (such as a punk hairstyle), a person with an Afro, a man with long hair, a man with his hair twisted up on the top of his head and covered with a turban, a man with long side curls, a person with long braids/dreadlocks, a person with a wig, and a person with a short, military-style haircut.

Discuss
Student Book p. 61

1. Answers will vary.
2. Answers will vary. Possible answers: Rock stars often try new or unusual hairstyles. These may include dying the hair different colors—sometimes bright or unusual colors—and cutting the hair in different shapes or even shaving it off. Teenagers and young adults sometimes try these new or unusual hairstyles, perhaps in less extreme forms.

Prepare
Student Book p. 61

Answers may vary. Possible answers:

1. The titles and subtitles suggest that the topic is questions and answers that people may have about hair—how long it grows and whether or not cutting it will make it grow faster.
2. Possible key facts about *hair* and *growth* (some may be true and some may be myths): Hair should be trimmed occasionally to keep it healthy and neat. Not trimming hair can cause the ends to split. Hair grows faster in the summer.
3. Pre-reading questions will vary. Possible questions:
   - Does hair grow faster or longer on some people than it does on others?
   - How many hairs are on a human head?

CHAPTER 4   **29**

Read
Student Book p. 62

Answers to the possible prediction questions from the *Prepare* section:
- Some people can grow their hair faster or longer than others; it depends on heredity (on their genes).
- The average human head has about 100,000 to 150,000 hairs.

Read Again
Student Book p. 62

Practice of individual reading strategies should be encouraged; answers will vary.

Students should identify the key sentence(s) in each paragraph as follows:

Paragraph 1: To answer this question, we have to find out how long the average hair is active. (The first sentence is the key sentence because the paragraph's main purpose is to describe average hair. However, sentences 1 and 9 together are also possible.)

Paragraph 2: Many people believe that cutting their hair makes it grow faster, thicker, and more luxuriant. However, this is not true.

For connectors (pronouns) and referents, see *C. Following Ideas* on TM page 30.

Signal words and predictions:
- *And* (lines 3, 6, 7, 10) indicates additional information.
- *Therefore* (line 4) indicates an effect or result.
- *However* (lines 4, 7) indicates contrasting information.
- *Also* (line 10) indicates additional information.

Post-Reading Activities

A. Comprehension Check

1. **a.** 0.35mm **b.** 500 to 1,800 **c.** The maximum length of scalp hair
2. Some people have very, very long hair because they have genes for longer hair.
3. The purpose of the experiments was to prove that cutting hair does not make it grow faster.
4. The steps in the scientists' experiments were as follows.
   a. They asked people to shave off the hair on one side of their heads.
   b. They collected the hair and measured it.
   c. They measured the hair left on the people's heads.
   d. They learned that hair growth was the same on both sides.

B. Vocabulary Check

Answers for some categories, such as "Can I guess or should I look in a dictionary?" will vary. Some sections of the chart may be completed as follows:

Word	Is it important?	Is there an internal definition?	Meaning
1. average	Yes (The word appears in a topic sentence.)	No	The amount that is typical for a group.
2. scalp	Yes (The word repeats.)	No	The part of the head that is covered with hair; hair grows on the scalp.
3. heredity	Yes (The idea is restated in the next sentence.)	Yes (line 6) Restatement: *Some people have genes for short hair; others grow hair much longer.*	Qualities or characteristics passed down through genes, from members of one family generation to the next.

Word	Is it important?	Is there an internal definition?	Meaning
4. maximum	Yes (The word is used in the explanation of a result.)	No	The highest amount possible.
5. genes	Yes (A related word is used.)	Yes (line 5) Related word: *heredity*	Information on DNA or RNA that determines what traits or features we will have.
6. luxuriant	Yes (It's a description word, but it appears in a topic sentence, and the idea is contrasted with the information that follows it.)	No	Lush, shows a lot of growth, abundant.
7. follicles	No (There is no internal definition, the word doesn't repeat, and the main idea is clear without full understanding of the term.)	No	The roots of hairs; where the hair grows from.
8. prove	Yes (A similar word is used.)	Yes (line 10) Similar word: *showed*	Use evidence (examples) and reasoning to show that something is true; make people believe something.
9. shave off	Yes (The word is used in a key step in a process of an experiment.)	No	Completely remove hair.
10. collected	No	No	Gathered, took all of something.

Choices of additional unfamiliar words will vary. Possible unfamiliar, important words: abbreviations for units of measurement: *mm (millimeter), cm (centimeter), km (kilometer).*

C. Following Ideas

The pronoun reference chart should be completed as follows:

Pronoun	Line	Refers to
1. we	1	X (subject pronoun; here, *we* means people in general; no referent)
2. them	4	hairs
3. it	7	hair (OR) their hair

D. Predicting Ideas with Signal Words

1. a. however — lines 1, 7
   b. therefore = line 4
2. a. however — predicts contrasting information
   b. therefore = predicts a conclusion or result
3. a. however = (line 4) contrasts (connects) the idea that generally, a total of about 9 km of hair grows each year with the fact that some people are able to grow their hair much longer
   = (line 7) contrasts (connects) the idea that people believe that cutting their hair makes it grow faster, thicker, and more luxuriant with the fact that it is not true; hair is dead
   b. therefore = connects the idea that the average head has about 100,000 to 150,000 hairs, of which about 80% are growing at the same time with the conclusion that a total of about 9 km of hair grows each year

Remember
Student Book p. 64

Illustrations may vary. Illustrations might show the following facts: Each hair usually grows for 500 to 1,800 days; scalp hair grows between 0.3 to 0.35 mm a day; the maximum length of scalp hair is between 20 and 60 cm; the average head has about 100,000 to 150,000 hairs; 80% of hairs are growing at the same time.

Discuss
Student Book p. 64

Answers will vary. Possible answers:

1. Baldness may be caused by age, heredity, illness (some autoimmune disorders cause baldness), and radiation treatments for cancer.
2. One famous product that is advertised as a stimulant for hair growth is Rogaine.™ It can be used for men or women. There are also shampoos that are said to stimulate hair growth. Additionally, some people have surgical procedures (hair transplants or hair plugs).

Prepare
Student Book p. 65

Answers may vary. Possible answers:

1. The title and subtitles suggest that this reading is about things you can do for your hair with products from your own kitchen. It may talk about simple ways you can improve the health and appearance of your hair.
2. Possible foods that could be used on hair: yogurt, eggs, lemon, tea, olive oil.
3. Pre-reading questions will vary. Possible questions:
   - How can I make my hair shine?
   - How can I make my hair less oily?
   - How can I make my hair less dry?
   - How can I dye my hair blond, or make my hair look blonder?

Read
Student Book p. 65

Answers to the possible prediction questions from the *Prepare* section:

- You can make hair shine by massaging an egg into clean and wet hair, by massaging mayonnaise into your hair and leaving it in overnight, and by rinsing your hair in beer in the shower.
- You can make hair less oily by rinsing your hair with a tablespoon of vinegar.

32 CHAPTER 4

- You can make hair less dry by massaging olive oil into your hair, covering your hair with plastic and a warm towel, and leaving it in for 30 minutes.
- You can brighten blond hair by rinsing your hair with lemon juice. (However, this is probably not strong enough to dye the hair.)

Read Again

Student Book p. 66

Practice of individual reading strategies should be encouraged; answers will vary.

Possible additional questions and answers:

Question: Are hair-care products from the kitchen as good as expensive commercial products?

Answer: In many cases, they are made from similar ingredients, so the kitchen products are as good as the commercial ones.

Question: Why does vinegar help oily hair?

Answer: Vinegar helps to remove the oil and grease.

For connectors (pronouns) and referents, see *C. Following Ideas* on TM page 34.

Signal words and predictions:

- *But* (line 2) indicates contrasting information.
- *And* (lines 5, 6, 11, 18, 23, 26) indicates additional information.
- *In the morning* (lines 13–14) indicates time or chronology of events.
- *Also* (line 17) indicates additional information.
- *After* (line 33) indicates time or chronology of events.

Post-Reading Activities

A. Comprehension Check

The chart of food problems and solutions may be completed as follows:

Problem	Solution
1. dry hair	Heat half a cup of olive oil. Massage it through your hair. Wrap your hair in plastic. Cover it with a warm towel. Wait for 30 minutes. Wash the oil out with a shampoo for dry hair.
2. oily hair	Whenever you wash your hair, put a tablespoon of vinegar in the rinse water.
3. hair that doesn't shine	Beat an egg and massage it into clean, wet hair. After five minutes, rinse it out with cool (not hot) water. Or rinse you hair in beer in the shower and then rinse it out with water.
4. damaged hair	Massage mayonnaise into your hair. Put a plastic bag on your head and keep the mayonnaise in your hair overnight. In the morning, rinse it out in cool water.

B. Vocabulary Check

1. a. advice b. ends
2. a. Egg for shine
   1. Beat an egg.
   2. Massage it into clean, wet hair.
   3. Wait five minutes.
   4. Rinse it out with cool water.

   b. Olive oil for dry hair
   1. Heat half a cup of olive oil.
   2. Massage it through your hair.
   3. Wrap your hair in plastic and a warm towel.
   4. Wait for 30 minutes.
   5. Wash the oil out carefully with a shampoo for dry hair.

3. The terms that are NOT foods and should be circled are: *massages, pillows, squeeze, towels*.

4. Answers for some categories, such as "Can I guess or should I look in a dictionary?" will vary. Some sections of the chart may be completed as follows:

Word	Is it important?	Is there an internal definition?	Meaning
1. conditioning	Yes (It appears in a topic sentence.)	Yes (line 16) *This is good for damaged hair.*	Using products to make your hair healthy and shiny.
2. overnight	Yes (It is a specific part of the instructions, telling readers how long to do something.)	No	All night (from when you go to bed to when you get up in the morning).
3. shine	Yes (It appears in the subtitle and the word repeats.)	No	Gleam, reflect the light, show color and brilliance.
4. oil	Yes (It appears in the subtitle, in a different form, and the word repeats.)	Yes (line 23) Similar word: *grease*	A liquid substance; not dry; similar to grease.
5. grease	Yes (It helps to define a related word.)	Yes (line 22 and subtitle) Similar word: *oil*	A liquid substance; not dry; similar to oil.
6. brighten	Yes (It appears in a topic sentence.)	No	To make more bright; to make a color more vivid, more noticeable.
7. roots	Yes (It is a specific part of instructions, telling where to start massaging the lemon juice into the hair.)	Yes (line 32) Opposite word: *tips*	The beginning of a hair, where it grows from the follicle.

Choices of additional unfamiliar words will vary.
Possible unfamiliar, important words: *beat, massage, rinse, scrambled, vinegar, liter, thoroughly*.

34 CHAPTER 4

C. Following Ideas

The pronoun reference chart should be completed as follows:

Pronoun	Line	Refers to
1. it	7	an egg
2. it	25	olive oil
3. it	26	your hair
4. it	31	the water (the liter of warm water with lemons)

D. Predicting Ideas with Signal Words

Answers may vary. Possible answers:

1. Use hot water, and you will have scrambled egg in your hair!
   (OR) Do not use hot water because you will have scrambled egg in your hair!
   (OR) Use cool water. As a result, you won't have scrambled egg in your hair.

2. Put a plastic bag on your head; otherwise, you will get mayonnaise on your pillow.
   (OR) Put a plastic bag on your head because you can get mayonnaise on your pillow.
   (OR) Put a plastic bag on your head. As a result, you won't get mayonnaise on your pillow.

3. Use a beer that doesn't smell too strong; otherwise, people may get the wrong idea.
   (OR) Don't use a beer that smells too strong because people may get the wrong idea.

Remember
Student Book p. 68

Illustrations will vary. Students may draw people doing two procedures in the article, possibly showing each step in a separate panel or box.

Discuss
Student Book p. 68
Answers will vary.

Prepare
Student Book p. 68

Answers may vary. Possible answers:

1. b. a poor person who succeeded in business (Reading the title and subtitle and scanning the topic sentences give us this information.)
2. The most important question this reading will answer is: How did this uneducated black woman become one of the wealthiest people in the United States?

Read
Student Book p. 69

Answer to the possible prediction question from the *Prepare* section:

- Madam C.J. Walker became one of the wealthiest people in the U.S. because she invented a cure for baldness in the form of a hair cream for African Americans. She started her own business, opened a school, and became rich.

Read Again
Student Book p. 69

Practice of individual reading strategies should be encouraged; answers will vary.

Possible additional questions and answers:

Question: Why did Madam C.J. Walker become interested in hair care?
Answer: She became interested in hair care because she was losing her hair.

Question: How did she get started in the hair care business?
Answer: She got started with a single hair cream that helped her hair grow.

Connectors (pronouns) and referents:

- *She* (lines 2, 4, 6, 12, 13, 15, 18, 25, 27, 35, 39, 44) refers to Madam C. J. Walker.
- *Her* (lines 4, 16, 19, 23, 25, 29, 42, 43, 44) refers to Madam C. J. Walker.
- *Their* (line 10) refers to African Americans.
- *They* (lines 10, 11) refers to African Americans.

- *Herself* (lines 11, 39) refers to Madam C.J. Walker
- *It* (line 17) refers to the hair cream Walker developed.
- *Them* (line 17) refers to other people.
- *They* (line 28) refers to the thousands of women studying at Walker's school.
- *Their* (line 30) refers to the thousands of women studying at Walker's school.

Signal words and predictions:
- *And* (lines 3, 11, 21, 25, 36, 41) indicates additional information.
- *However* (lines 5, 23) indicates contrasting information.
- *By the time* (lines 5–6) indicates time or chronology of events.
- *At the time* (line 9) indicates time or chronology of events.
- *Because* (line 10) indicates a reason or cause.
- *Then* (lines 16, 29) indicates time or chronology of events.
- *Within a few years* (lines 19–20) indicates time or chronology of events.
- *In addition* (line 24) indicates additional information.
- *After* (line 28) indicates time or chronology of events.
- *Finally* (line 34) indicates conclusion.
- *Also* (line 39) indicates additional information.

Post-Reading Activities

A. Comprehension Check

The events of C. J. Walker's life should appear in the following order:

- __1__ Her parents died.
- __2__ She got married.
- __3__ She had a baby.
- __4__ Her husband died.
- __5__ She had a strange dream.
- __6__ She made hair cream.
- __7__ She tested the hair cream.
- __8__ She started a business.
- __9__ She became very rich.

B. Vocabulary Check

1. a. businesswomen = women who run their own businesses or who work in a business

   b. deathbed = the bed that somebody dies in

   c. washerwoman = a woman who washes clothes/does laundry for a living

2. The chart should be completed as follows:

Adjective	Noun
1. poor	poverty
2. rich	riches
3. wealthy	wealth

3. Answers for some categories, such as "Can I guess or should I look in a dictionary?" will vary. Some sections of the chart may be completed as follows:

Word	Is it important?	Is there an internal definition?	Meaning
1. orphan	No (The word does not repeat, and is not key to the main idea of the reading.)	No	Someone whose parents have died.
2. widow	No (The word does not repeat, and is not key to the main idea of the reading.)	No	A woman whose husband has died.

36 CHAPTER 4

Word	Is it important?	Is there an internal definition?	Meaning
3. formula	Yes (The word repeats.)	No	A recipe or a method for making something.
4. cream	Yes (The word repeats.)	No	An ointment or liquid that can be rubbed into the hair or the skin.
5. achievement	Yes (The word repeats, and it appears in both a topic sentence and the last line of the reading.)	No	Success, accomplishment.
6. unskilled	No (It's a description word.)	No	Lacking certain skills or training that can be used for a job.
7. generous	Yes (The word repeats, and it appears in a topic sentence.)	Yes (lines 35–36) Related word and idea: *gave a great deal of money*	Giving; unselfish.
8. causes	Yes (The word appears in a topic sentence.)	Yes (lines 36–38) Examples: *black colleges and organizations that were fighting for the rights of black people*	Social issues that concern a group of people–usually issues or concerns involving unfair or unequal treatment, which people want to see changed.
9. a great deal of	No (These are description words.)	No	A lot of, a large amount of.
10. mansions	No (It's an item in a list.)	No	Very large, elegant, and expensive houses.

Choices of additional unfamiliar words will vary. Possible unfamiliar, important words: *empress, received, cure, baldness, employing, graduated, rights.*

C. Predicting Ideas with Signal Words

1. a. finally = line 34
   b. however = lines 5, 23
   c. in addition = line 24

2. a. finally = shows the last item in a sequence of events or points—in this case, a sequence of information about C. J. Walker's life. It connects the last idea of the previous paragraph (*At a time when most black women worked as maids, cooks, washerwomen, or unskilled factory workers, C. J. Walker had great wealth*) with a new point about Walker's life (*She was also generous to African-American causes*).
   Possible restatement: In addition to being very wealthy, C. J. Walker gave a lot of money to organizations that supported African-American concerns.

   b. however = (line 5) connects the following two contrasting facts about C. J. Walker's life: *She spent much of her early working life as a washerwoman* and *By the time Walker*

CHAPTER 4   37

died in 1919, she was one of the wealthiest women in the United States.
Possible restatement: Although she spent much of her early working life as a washerwoman, by the time she died in 1919, she was one of the wealthiest women in the United States.

= (line 23) appears at the end of a sentence, but it also highlights contrasting information about Walker. Rephrasing the sentence shows how it connects these ideas: Walker developed a cure for baldness. However, this may not have been her greatest achievement.
Possible restatement: Walker developed a cure for baldness. However, she had an even greater achievement by employing hundreds of black men and women in her company and helping thousands of women become successful businesswomen.

c. in addition = predicts additional information—in this case, about C. J. Walker's achievements. It connects the following ideas: *She employed hundreds of black men and women in her company* and *She helped thousands of women become successful businesswomen.*
Possible restatement: She employed hundreds of black men and women in her company, and she also helped thousands of women become successful businesswomen.

Remember
Student Book p.71

Timelines may vary. Possible timeline:

1867	1874	1881	1884	1887	?	?	?	?	1919
Born	Parents died	Married	Had child	Widowed	Dreamed about hair cream	Developed and tested cream	Traveled and sold cream, ran business	Opened a school	Died

Discuss
Student Book p. 71

Answers will vary. Possible answers:

1. One successful entrepreneur today is Calvin Klein, who has a clothing fashion empire. Klein had little money when he began, but he is now one of the most successful designers in the world. Another entrepreneur is Bill Gates, the CEO of Microsoft. He was a college dropout, but he bought a computer operating system and developed a company.

2. Many companies, large or small, have failed in the high tech industry. Many dot.com (Internet) companies, start-ups that were popular in the 1990s, did not last. Larger companies have also failed in recent years (Polaroid, Digital...). Some people say that many dot.com start up companies failed because of poor management (they were often run by very young people), or because there were too many of them and they did not anticipate people losing interest in buying things off of the Internet—the demand was suddenly no longer there. Larger companies may have failed for financial reasons, and the difficulty of keeping people interested in their products.

Reading Skills and Strategies

Prepare

Making Predictions about the Text
Student Book p. 73

ACTIVITY 1

Answers may vary. Possible answers:

Features: Name and title of author (M.D. = medical doctor), long sentences with facts about low-density lipoprotein and heart disease, acronyms (such as "LDL") and complex vocabulary

Predictions:
- Content: Facts. The article will give information about low-density lipoprotein and heart disease. It may define some key words. It will talk about a health issue. It may present recent findings from research.
- Genre: Magazine (scholarly—medical journal?) or report
- Purpose: Inform, give news about this development in medical research
- Audience: Experts/medical professionals/scientists (The article is written by a medical doctor, and the article contains a lot of specialized terms.)
- Difficulty: Difficult

ACTIVITY 2

Answers may vary. Possible answers:

1. **Britain Tries to Save the Basking Shark**

   Features: Author's name and position (newspaper correspondent), date, art (graph showing statistics), beginning of an article

   Predictions:
   - Genre: Newspaper or magazine, but probably a newspaper because of the date
   - Audience: General adult readers
   - Content: Facts, explanations. The article may discuss facts about the basking shark, whose numbers are decreasing, and what Britain is doing to save this species of shark. It may talk about different ways that Britain is trying to save the shark through new environmental laws. It may discuss reasons for why the shark is declining.
   - Difficulty: Probably not very difficult

2. **Save the Basking Shark!**

   Features: Exclamation points in the title and in some of the sentences (informal), direct question as the first sentence, fun illustration (not realistic) of a shark

   Predictions:
   - Genre: Kids' magazine
   - Content: Facts and opinions. The article may discuss facts about the basking shark and reasons why it is in trouble in Britain. It may also tell readers what they can do to help save the shark, and it may try to persuade them to take some kind of action.
   - Difficulty: Not very difficult
   - Audience: Kids, probably ages 10–14

3. **Basking Shark**

   Features: Title and subtitles and science "family" categories; no author name given; complex, specialized vocabulary (scientific); long, complex sentences; lots of information.

   Predictions:
   - Genre: Textbook
   - Content: Facts, explanations. This reading will probably give scientific facts about the

basking shark—how it is related to other kinds of sharks, and where it is found in the world.
- Audience: Learners (could include adults and teens), groups with a special interest in sharks or in marine biology

Read

Identifying the Main Idea
Student Book p. 78

ACTIVITY 3

1. People who live in modern houses have many important services that they do not even think about.
2. This latter state is called the balance of nature.
3. The Romans were the first great road builders in Europe.
4. Implied topic sentence: Italians may have different values.

Using Connectors to Follow Ideas
Student Book p. 80

ACTIVITY 4

1. That = you won the scholarship (you winning the scholarship)
2. there = the state university
3. those = the eggs
4. then = that semester

ACTIVITY 5

Advise students that some connectors may refer to or imply a person/thing not specified in the sentence.

1. one = school record
2. That = the money; you = Phil
3. There = X (no referent; it's the subject of the sentence); there = the woods
4. That = no one knew where John went; they = the people who didn't know where John went
5. a few = books
6. one = X (no referent, but implies people in general); then = when I first learned to drive
7. There = Mars; it = the spaceship
8. The giraffe = the strangest animal
9. you = the building manager; this policy = not allowing pets in the elevator; that = X (no referent; part of a noun clause); It's = X (no referent; subject pronoun for the sentence); we = X (no referent, but implies building management); one = a pet

Using Signal Words to Predict Ideas
Student Book p. 82

ACTIVITY 6

1. b. Young birds cannot fly
2. a. He often wears strange clothing
3. c. We won't have time to visit her
4. b. You didn't buy sugar at the grocery store
5. b. She never gets to meetings on time
6. c. I had many reasons to quit school

ACTIVITY 7

The events should be ordered as follows:

1	John bought a car.
2	He got his first paycheck.
3	He lost his job.
4	He returned the car to the dealer.
5	The dealer made him pay extra money.
6	He was upset.
7	He found a better job.
8	He got a raise.
9	He got a really good car.

Remember

Using Graphic Organizers
Student Book p. 84

ACTIVITY 8

1. Simple timeline 2. Flowchart 3. Cluster diagram 4. Block diagram 5. Flowchart

Using Grammar
Student Book p. 86

ACTIVITY 9

Answers may vary. Possible answers:

1. what repairman used > noun > names things—a tool?
2. *high school* describes it > object of preposition *until* > noun > names things—an event? A kind of party where people who went to school together meet again?
3. describes adjectives *more beautiful* > says how or how much more beautiful > very, very much? extremely?
4. object of preposition *in* > is preceded by article *the* > noun > names things > a group of people who sing together?
5. follows a verb that is similar to the verb *be* > describes noun (Mary) > adjective > extremely frightened? out of control?
6. comes before a noun > describes the noun > adjective > a flavor or a certain style of cooking from another culture? (Indian)
7. follows a noun subject > describes an action, what something does > verb > increased?
8. is the subject of a sentence, preceding a verb > names a thing > noun > a type of medicine or treatment?
9. is the object of the verb *use* > is preceded by the article *a* > names a thing > noun > a special device or instrument to help put on a shoe?

Using Word Forms
Student Book p. 88

ACTIVITY 10

1. undriveable = not driveable, not able to be driven (prefix *un-* = not; suffix *-able* = adjective)
2. repaint = paint again (prefix *re-* = again; paint = verb)
3. saddened = made people feel sad (suffix *-en* = verb; suffix *-ed* = past tense of the verb)
4. penniless = without a penny, without any money, broke (suffix *-less* = without, and *-less* = adjective)
5. problematic = causes problems, difficult, complicated (suffix *-ic* = adjective)
6. unimportant = not important (prefix *un-* = not; suffix *-ant* = adjective)
7. chemist = a person who works in the field of chemistry (suffix *-ist* = noun, indicating a person who works in a certain field or area of study)
8. builder = a person who builds something (suffix *-er* = noun, a person who does a certain job or activity)

CHAPTER 5   41

Using World Knowledge
Student Book p. 90

ACTIVITY 11

Answers will vary. Possible answers/guesses of word meanings:

1. reevaluating = evaluating again, considering again, rethinking, trying to do differently (Sample use of world knowledge to guess: I failed a class once. I realized that the way I was studying was not working. I had to try something new in order to do better the next time.)

2. pugilist = a fighter, someone who fights someone else in sports like boxing or martial arts (Sample use of world knowledge to guess: I have seen movies with Jackie Chan. Jackie Chan does kung fu. He is often fighting against someone using this martial art in his movies.)

3. canoe = a type of boat; a long, narrow boat; people usually use paddles to move and steer it (Sample use of world knowledge to guess: I have seen pictures of Native Americans and the types of boats they used to travel down rivers and across lakes. I also went to a camp one summer where we learned how to use this type of boat.)

4. packs = groups of animals (Sample use of world knowledge to guess: In the sentence, wolves and cats are contrasted; cats hunt alone, but wolves don't. Also, I have seen pictures of and TV shows about wolves, and I have seen how they hunt together.)

5. narrowed = became smaller, less wide (Sample use of world knowledge to guess: The sentence itself gives the meaning—if there is only room for one person, the cave is narrow, not wide. But I also remember on a hiking trip I went on, there were signs warning us that the path would narrow. At first, six of us could walk comfortably together, but when the path became smaller, we had to walk single file.)

6. whined = complained (Sample use of world knowledge to guess: I used to babysit my younger sisters and cousins, and I know that children complain a lot about bedtimes and other things. The word has a negative idea.)

ACTIVITY 12

Answers may vary. Possible choices and explanations of important and unimportant words, and possible guesses of word meanings:

1. a. coloring = not important; item listed in a series

   b. handed down = important; explains the main idea from the topic sentence
   Possible meaning: passed down to through genes/heredity, transferred to, given to

   c. similarities = important; relates to the main idea as expressed in the topic sentence, and similar words are used throughout the paragraph
   Possible meaning: things that are similar; likenesses; common traits or features

   d. lasting = important; relates to the main idea; describes "lessons," which is a word that is repeated
   Possible meaning: enduring; something that lasts a long time

   e. unlearn = important; relates to the main idea, and appears in the last sentence
   Possible meaning: not learn; take away something you have already learned

2. a. Weston Handicap = not important; specific event name. (only important to know that it is an event)

   b. silks = not important; the main idea of the paragraph is to show how cold the person was, but we don't need to know specifically what this word means

   c. sleet = not important; not directly related to the main idea, and the word is used for a figurative comparison

   d. stable boys = not important; not directly related to the main idea about the cold temperatures at the event

   e. jockeys = important; we need to understand it to know what Pete does, and the word appears in the last sentence of the paragraph
   Possible meaning: a person who races horses

3. a. Anton van = important; subject of Leeuenhoek paragraph/story; names the person who got the vial from the lake, the famous naturalist and pioneer of microscopy

   b. respectable = important; adjective, description word

42 CHAPTER 5

Possible meaning: able to be respected by others; important; distinguished; people would believe what he said

c. dry-goods = not important; adjective, description word; tells us what kind of store, but the idea of the store is not related to the main idea of the paragraph

d. approached = important; relates to the main idea of the paragraph, what this man did at the lake
Possible meaning: came near; went to

e. vial = important; relates to the main idea of the paragraph, what this man did at the lake
Possible meaning: a small container (small enough to fit in his pocket); a type of bottle

Reading: Food on the Run

Getting Started
Student Book p. 92

1. Answers will vary.
2. Readings 3 and 4 are about fast-food restaurants in trouble.

Prepare
Student Book p. 93

Answers will vary. Possible answers:

1. The main features of the text are a title that looks like a newspaper headline or a report, the form with name, date, and class information that shows the writer is a student, and the name and date of the publication, the name and position of the author, and sentences that do not seem very long or complex. The article appears to be from a high school newspaper, or probably a class report.

   a. topic: how fast food developed in the United States.
   b. content type: facts, explanations
   c. audience: teacher(s) and students/classmates
   d. difficulty: not very difficult

2. Possible terms related to *fast food* and *businesses*: service, convenience, cheap, inexpensive, efficient, franchise, chain, costs, industry, sales.

3. Pre-reading questions will vary. Possible questions:
   • When did fast food begin?
   • How many fast-food restaurants are there in the U.S. today?

Read
Student Book p. 93

Answers to the possible prediction questions from the *Prepare* section:

• Fast food began in the U.S. in 1916.
• There are around 160,000 fast-food restaurants in the U.S. today.

Read Again
Student Book p. 95

Practice of individual reading strategies should be encouraged; answers will vary.

Possible additional questions and answers:

Question: What was the first fast-food restaurant chain in the United States?
Answer: The first fast-food restaurant chain was called White Castle.

Question: What is one of the most successful fast-food restaurants?

Answer: McDonald's is one of the most successful ones.

For connectors and referents, see *C. Following Ideas* on TM page 45.

Signal words and predictions:

- *100 years ago* (line 1) indicates time or chronology of events.
- *However* (line 2) indicates contrasting information.
- *After* (lines 3, 4) indicates time or chronology of events.
- *In (year)* (lines 4, 15, 19, 21, 22) indicates time or chronology of events.
- *And* (lines 4, 8, 9, 12, 15, 19, 23, 25) indicates additional information.
- *First* (line 9) indicates time or chronology of events.
- *Then* (line 10) indicates time or chronology of events.
- *Therefore* (line 11) indicates an effect or result.
- *In fact* (line 13) indicates emphasis.
- *In that year* (line 17) indicates time or chronology of events.
- *At the end of 1957* (line 18) indicates time or chronology of events.
- *By* (lines 18, 23) indicates time or chronology of events.
- *Such as* (line 25) indicates an example.

Post-Reading Activities

A. Comprehension Check

1916:	The first fast-food chain, White Castle, opened.
1948:	Richard and Maurice McDonald started a hamburger stand in San Bernardino, California.
1953:	The McDonald brothers decided to franchise their successful business. McDonald's franchises opened in Arizona and California.
1954:	A salesman named Ray Kroc started selling franchises for the McDonald brothers.
1957:	There were 37 McDonald's franchises.
1959:	There were over 100 McDonald's franchises.
1961:	Kroc bought the McDonald's corporation from the McDonald brothers and began building restaurants all over the United States.
1962:	Dave Thomas opened the first Wendy's restaurant.

B. Vocabulary Check

Answers for some categories (such as whether or not world knowledge may be used) may vary. Some sections of the chart may be completed as follows:

Word	Is it important?	Is there an internal definition?	It is a noun? verb? adjective?
1. chain	Yes (The word repeats.)	No	Noun
2. Castle	No (The word is part of the name of a restaurant.)	No	Noun (name of a place)
3. cheaply	Yes (The word is related to the main idea, and synonyms are repeated.)	Yes (line 6) Synonym: *inexpensive*	Adverb
4. inexpensive	Yes (The word is related to the main idea, and synonyms are repeated.)	Yes (line 5) Synonym: *cheaply*	Adjective

Word	Is it important?	Is there an internal definition?	It is a noun? verb? adjective?
5. stand	Yes (It is related to the main idea, and a synonym is repeated.)	Yes (lines 8,9,10) Similar word: *restaurant*	
6. economical	Yes (The word repeats.)	Yes (line 8) *Reduced costs*	Adjective
7. efficient	Yes (The word repeats.)	Yes (line 10) *They needed to make food more quickly*	Adjective
8. simplify	Yes (The word helps to explain a main idea in the article.)	Yes (lines 11–12) Restatement: *They served only a few items.*	Verb
9. franchise	Yes (The word repeats.)	Yes (lines 14–15) *This meant that people would pay the McDonald brothers a fee in order to build restaurants according to the McDonald design.*	Noun and verb
10. fee	Yes (It is part of the explanation of another key word, *franchise*.)	No	Noun
11. growth	Yes (The word appears in the title and in a topic sentence.)	No	Noun
12. brilliant	No (The word is an adjective or description word.)	No	Adjective
13. encourage	Yes (It relates to the topic sentence of the paragraph on lines 20–21.)	No	Verb

Choices of additional unfamiliar words will vary. Possible unfamiliar, important words: *diet, stand, industries, billion.*

C. Following Ideas

The reference chart should be completed as follows:

Word	Line	Refers to
1. the brothers	5	Richard and Maurice McDonald
2. this	14	franchising the restaurants
3. there	18	X (subject of a sentence; no referent)
4. these businesses	22–23	Burger King and Wendy's

D. Predicting Ideas with Signal Words

1. The following signal words should be underlined in each sentence:
   a. First b. The next step c. Soon

All of these signal words/phrases show time order.

2. Predictions may vary. Answers are as follows:
   a. The McDonald brothers reduced costs to make their restaurant economical.
   b. McDonald's franchises opened in Arizona and California.
   c. Other fast-food chains opened and spread throughout the United States.

E. Identifying the Main Idea

Paragraph 1: Fast food began in the United States fewer than 100 years ago.

Paragraph 2: In 1948, three years after the end of the war, Richard and Maurice McDonald decided to start a different kind of fast-food restaurant.

Paragraph 3: They knew that their restaurant had to be economical and efficient.

Paragraph 4: In fact, the McDonald restaurant was so successful that the brothers decided to franchise their restaurants.

Paragraph 5: The next step in the growth of McDonald's came in 1954.

Paragraph 6: With more than $65 billion in sales per year, fast food is one of the most successful American industries.

Remember
Student Book p. 97

Exercise A (*Comprehension Check*) uses a timeline as a graphic organizer.

The topic "How to make a profit from an inexpensive product" could also be charted as a block diagram. Possible diagram:

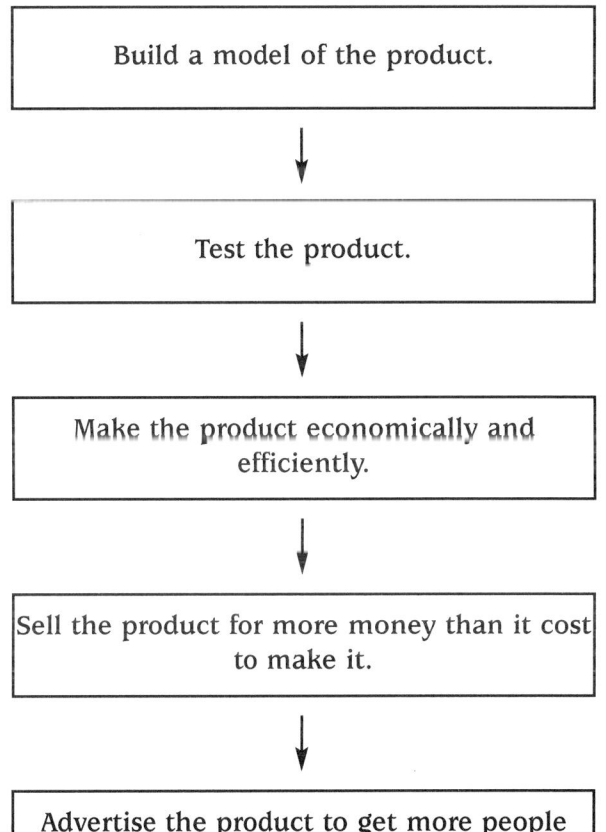

Discuss
Student Book p. 97

1. Answers will vary.
2. Answers may vary. Possible answers: The author of the article may have written about fast food because he likes to eat it, he works in the fast-food industry, he knows that people (especially high school students) eat fast food and might be interested in the history of it, or he might want to open his own franchise someday—he might be interested in business. Other topics about fast food that might interest his audience could be as follows: Is fast food really bad for you? Are their healthy options in fast-food restaurants? How often do Americans eat fast food?

Prepare
Student Book p. 97

Answers may vary. Possible answers:

1. The information is ordered in the form of charts, or tables.
2. The charts can be read horizontally (in rows) and vertically (in columns). You can find the type of information you want to read for and then read across and down to find the statistic in the chart. The charts give the following kinds of information:
   Chart 1: The nutritional needs of adult men and women—the maximum and minimum amounts of things that they can have.
   Chart 2: The nutritional information for different pieces of chicken in the Kentucky Fried Chicken recipe.
   Chart 3: The nutritional information for different types of food offered at McDonald's restaurants.
3. Possible terms related to fast-food menus and nutrition: *calories, grams, fat, sodium, cholesterol, carbohydrates, fiber, protein, vitamins, sugar, serving size, healthy, unhealthy.*

4. Pre-reading questions will vary. Possible questions about each chart:
   Chart 1
   - Who can have more calories per day—men or women?
   - Which nutritional needs are the same for men and women?
   Chart 2
   - Which piece of chicken has the largest serving size and the most calories?
   - Which chicken pieces contain vitamins?
   Chart 3
   - Which item on the McDonald's menu has the most calories?
   - Which item on the McDonald's menu has the least calories?

Read
Student Book p. 98

Answers to the possible prediction questions from the *Prepare* section:

Chart 1
- Men can have 500 more calories per day than women.
- Men and women have the same maximum amount of cholesterol and sodium.

Chart 2
- The chicken breast is the largest serving size, at 153 grams and 5.4 ounces; it has 400 calories, while all other pieces have fewer than 300.
- None of the chicken pieces contain vitamins. However, chicken breasts and thighs contain calcium and iron; whole wings and drumsticks contain iron.

Chart 3
- The McDonald's Big Mac has the most calories (580).
- The McDonald's side salad has the least calories (15).

Read Again
Student Book p. 99

Answers will vary, depending on students' pre-reading questions.

Post-Reading Activities

A. Comprehension Check

Answers may vary slightly. In reading the chart, students may determine what is healthy or unhealthy based primarily on the amount of calories. However, they should also be encouraged to look at other categories, such as sodium and cholesterol. Food with fewer calories may not be as healthy as it appears; it may be high in sodium or cholesterol, or low in nutritional content.

1. The healthiest meal at a fast-food restaurant is a 6-piece chicken McNuggets (though it is high in sodium, it is lower in calories), a small side salad, and lowfat milk or orange juice. Other healthy options might include chicken wings or drumsticks at Kentucky Fried Chicken—though again, these are high in sodium, they have fewer calories and calories from fat, and they are somewhat lower in cholesterol.

2. The unhealthiest meal at a fast-food restaurant is a Big Mac, large french fries, a Coca-Cola or Sprite, and a baked apple pie, at McDonald's. These food items have the highest amount of calories; they also have a great deal of sodium and low nutritional content. A close runner-up would be the sausage biscuit with egg at McDonald's, which has 480 calories and 1,010 mg of sodium. A Kentucky Fried Chicken chicken breast would also be an unhealthy meal.

B. Vocabulary Check

Answers may vary. Possible answers:

1. The most important nutritional terms on the charts are the following: *calories, fat, cholesterol, sodium, carbohydrate, fiber,* and *protein*. These terms appear as categories in more than one chart. Other terms that might be important to know are units of measurement and their abbreviations: *grams (g), milligrams (mg),* and *ounces*. Knowing the vocabulary of some of the food items on Charts 2 and 3 also could be important, since these items appear as categories.

2. Some ways to guess the meanings of items on the menu are as follows: For Chart 3, use world knowledge of different meals (breakfast, lunch, dessert, drinks) and think about the types of food that are served at these meals (sandwiches, meat items, sweet foods, etc.). Or think about things you have ordered in the past, at this restaurant or at other fast-food restaurants.

3. The charts are still useful even if you do not know the meaning of every term. Looking at the numbers gives an idea of which menu items are healthy or unhealthy. The main thing to be aware of is which items should have a low number (*calories, fat, cholesterol, sodium*) and which should have a higher number (*vitamins, calcium, iron, fiber*). In Chart 2, percentages are given for some of the food items, informing readers of the percent of the nutritional content compared with the recommended amount in a daily diet. Therefore, even if the reader does not know exactly what a gram, milligram, or ounce is, some information can still be interpreted.

Remember
Student Book p. 100

Graphic organizers may vary, but a chart is the most logical type to use for this activity. Students might create one chart including items and nutritional information from a menu for one meal (breakfast, lunch, or dinner) or for more than one meal. Students might even discuss which meal of the day would be healthiest at a fast-food restaurant for someone who is dieting.

Discuss
Student Book p. 100

Answers will vary. Possible answers:

1. Yes, fast-food restaurants should provide nutrition facts. The information needs to be easily accessible and visible. Most people don't realize how unhealthy some fast food is, and they might think twice about eating it—or they might order more carefully—if they knew. It is very unhealthy to be overweight, and people need to be educated about nutrition.
(OR) No, fast-food restaurants should not provide nutrition facts. Fast-food restaurants are businesses that employ many people, and these businesses have to survive. Many people can eat fast food occasionally and not have any health problems. Providing nutrition facts just

makes people too afraid, and most people don't know how to interpret the nutrition facts. How many people really know how many calories or how much sodium they should eat? Providing this information might scare away customers and hurt the businesses. If people really want to know what is in their food, they can always look for that information on the Internet or write to the company to get information.

2. People SHOULD NOT eat fast food because it is unhealthy. It is low in nutrition—it does not have as many vitamins as fresh food—and it is cooked with a lot of unhealthy grease. Fast food is cheap and convenient for many people, especially working parents with children; however, people become too dependent on it and put their health in danger. They can gain weight, which leads to other health problems. People should learn how to prepare meals at home that are economical, efficient, and healthy. **(OR)** People SHOULD eat fast food because it tastes good, it is convenient, and it is inexpensive. As long as you don't eat it all the time, it isn't bad for you. Many people don't have time to cook meals. Eating at more expensive restaurants isn't economical for many people. Eating fast food is better than not eating at all. Many people have very busy schedules, and a fast-food meal is all they have time for on their lunch break. Fast food is also a good option for students, who don't always have a lot of time or money, but they need to eat something to have energy for learning.

Prepare
Student Book p. 100

1. b. a man suing fast-food restaurants because of health problems (The title of the article gives us this information.)
2. c. a newspaper (A city name is given at the beginning of the article; also, there is a headline but no author.)
3. Possible terms related to the effects of eating fast food: *overweight, obese, high cholesterol, high fat, high blood pressure, diabetes.*

4. Prediction question in the student book: What kinds of health problems did Mr. Barber have? Possible additional questions:
   - Is Mr. Barber the only one with health problems from fast-food restaurants?
   - Will the lawsuit be successful?

Read
Student Book p. 101

Possible answer to the prediction question from the *Prepare* section:
- Mr. Barber's health problems include obesity, diabetes, high blood pressure, and two heart attacks.

Answers to the possible additional prediction questions from the *Prepare* section:
- Mr. Barber is not the only one who says that health problems resulted from fast-food restaurants; Frances Winn and Israel Bradley also have health problems.
- Some people say that the lawsuit won't be successful because some restaurants do offer healthy choices, and people are free to make their own choices.

Read Again
Student Book p. 101

Practice of individual reading strategies should be encouraged; answers will vary.

The main idea of each paragraph should be underlined as follows:

Paragraph 1: A man from New York is suing four big fast-food companies.

Paragraph 2: Barber's lawyer, Samuel Hirsch, says that the suit has two different purposes.

Paragraph 3: Two others may soon join Barber's suit.

Paragraph 4: Officials of the fast-food industry attacked the legal action.

Paragraph 5: Whether or not the suit is successful, there is no doubt that Americans have a weight problem.

For connectors and referents, see *C. Following Ideas* on TM page 50.

Post-Reading Activities

A. Comprehension Check

1. Caesar Barber is suing fast-food companies because he says that the high-fat foods they serve destroyed his health.
2. He wants the fast-food companies to offer healthier foods in smaller amounts and to provide warning labels similar to those on cigarettes.
3. According to Barber's lawyer, the effects of eating fast food are similar to the effects of cigarettes, alcohol, and illegal drugs such as heroin.
4. Fast-food companies think the suit is ridiculous. The spokeswoman for KFC says that her company offers healthy choices.

B. Vocabulary Check

1. There are several compound words in the article: *fast-food companies, fast-food restaurants, fast-food industry, high-fat foods, health problems, weight problem, warning labels*. *High-fat foods* are foods that are high in fat. *Health problems* are problems with health; a *weight problem* is being overweight. *Warning labels* are written warnings about the dangers of a product.
2. Synonym for *legal action*: suit.
3. Words with a suffix meaning "a person who or that which": *reporter, killer*.
4. Answers for some categories, such as "Can I use world knowledge?" will vary. Some sections of the chart may be completed as follows:

Word	Is it important?	Is there an internal definition?	It is a noun? verb? adjective?
1. suing	Yes (It appears in the title, topic sentences, and the first paragraph.)	Yes (lines 2–3) *going to court*	Verb (in progressive form)
2. obesity	Yes (The word repeats, in different forms.)	Yes (lines 7–8) *very overweight*	Noun (adjective = *obese*)
3. diabetes	Yes (The word repeats.)	No	Noun
4. illegal	No (The word appears only once, and is a description word for a noun not directly related to the main idea.)	Yes (line 31) Antonym: *legal*	Adjective
5. claims	Yes (The word repeats; also its synonym *says* repeats.)	Yes (line 5) Synonym: *says*	Verb
6. warning labels	Yes (The word repeats and is an important part of the main idea of the paragraph.)	No	Noun

50 CHAPTER 6

Word	Is it important?	Is there an internal definition?	It is a noun? verb? adjective?
7. attacked	Yes (It appears in a topic sentence.)	Yes (line 32) Restatement: *called it ridiculous*	Verb
8. ridiculous	Yes (It's a description word, but here it's important for understanding the main idea of the paragraph.)	No	Adjective

Choices of additional unfamiliar words will vary. Possible unfamiliar, important words: *court, heroin, representative, spokeswoman.*

C. Following Ideas

The reference chart should be completed as follows:

Word	Line	Refers to
1. these restaurants	6	McDonald's, Burger King, Wendy's, and KFC
2. this diet	7	(the fact that) he ate at these restaurants four or five times a week for many years
3. there	10	these restaurants (McDonald's, Burger King, Wendy's, and KFC)
4. this habit	24	eating at fast-food restaurants at least twice a week since 1975
5. they	40	medical experts

D. Identifying the Main Idea

Paragraph 2: Barber's lawyer, Samuel Hirsch, says that the suit has two different purposes.

Paragraph 3: Two others may soon join Barber's suit.

Paragraph 4: Officials of the fast-food industry attacked the legal action.

CHAPTER 6 51

Remember
Student Book p. 103

Information in graphic organizers may vary. The most logical graphic organizer to use is a block diagram. Possible diagram:

```
┌─────────────────────────────────────┐
│ Caesar Barber was single and not    │
│ a very good cook, so he ate at      │
│ fast-food restaurants.              │
└─────────────────────────────────────┘
                 ↓
┌─────────────────────────────────────┐
│ Caesar Barber ate at fast-food      │
│ restaurants four or five times a    │
│ week for many years.                │
└─────────────────────────────────────┘
                 ↓
┌─────────────────────────────────────┐
│ He became very overweight.          │
└─────────────────────────────────────┘
                 ↓
┌─────────────────────────────────────┐
│ His obesity caused his diabetes,    │
│ high blood pressure, and two heart  │
│ attacks.                            │
└─────────────────────────────────────┘
                 ↓
┌─────────────────────────────────────┐
│ He sued four big fast-food          │
│ companies, saying that they were    │
│ responsible for his health problems.│
└─────────────────────────────────────┘
                 ↓
┌─────────────────────────────────────┐
│ Other people who ate fast food for  │
│ many years may also join the suit.  │
└─────────────────────────────────────┘
```

Discuss
Student Book p. 103

1. Answers will vary.
   Possible agreement with Mr. Barber: Mr. Barber should sue these companies. There was no information given to him about the risks to his health. He has suffered a lot from eating this food. There are many people like him who eat at fast-food restaurants a lot because it is convenient. He should sue the companies to help bring public attention to this important issue.
   Possible disagreement with Mr. Barber: Mr. Barber's health problems are unfortunate, but the fast-food companies are not responsible. Mr. Barber should have known that it was not healthy to eat so much fast food so often. He could have gone on a diet or changed his eating habits when he first became overweight. Why did he continue eating fast food even after he had other health problems? Why didn't he start learning about nutrition and fast-food health risks when he first became overweight?

2. Answers will vary.

Prepare
Student Book p. 103

Answers may vary. Possible answers:

1. The topic of the letters is the spread of fast-food restaurants like McDonald's in foreign countries. The two writers seem to have different opinions about this.

2. Features of the text: Title and date of the publication (it's a newspaper), title of the section in which the letters appear, author's initials or names but no title or position. Sentences are not long or complex, and there are no specialized terms. There are no illustrations or charts. Based on these features, the following predictions might be made.
   a. genre: newspaper editorials (letters to the editor)
   b. audience: adult readers (possible adult readers in a foreign country)
   c. purpose: to show two different opinions about fast-food restaurants abroad; possibly to persuade readers to agree with one opinion over the other
   d. difficulty: not very difficult

52   CHAPTER 6

3. Possible words and phrases associated with *fast-food restaurants* and their effects on foreign countries: *profits, abroad, local, regional, disappear, Americanize, adapt, culture, spread, increase.*

4. The first letter might say something critical or negative about American fast-food restaurants increasing in foreign countries. It might suggest that these restaurants are taking away from the food and culture of those places. The second letter might say something about how these American businesses are not responsible, and that the criticism is unfair.
   - Possible question for Letter 1: How many American fast-food restaurants are doing business in other countries?
   - Possible question for Letter 2: Why are American fast-food restaurants not to blame?

Read
Student Book p. 104

Answers to the possible prediction questions from the *Prepare* section:

- Letter 1: There are more than 8,000 McDonald's restaurants in 101 countries.
- Letter 2: American fast-food restaurants have changed their menus to fit the tastes of people in those countries. Additionally, the owners of the businesses are not Americans, and nobody is making people eat there.

Read Again
Student Book p. 105

Practice of individual reading strategies should be encouraged; answers will vary.

The main idea of each letter should be underlined as follows:

Letter 1: People around the world may not know it, but our cultures are in danger. It is from American fast food.

Letter 2: The writer claimed that American fast-food restaurants are destroying cultures around the world. In my opinion, this is totally untrue.

For connectors and referents, see *C. Following Ideas* on TM page 54.

Signal words and predictions:

- *But* (line 1) indicates contrasting information.
- *In (year)* (line 9) indicates time or chronology of events.
- *By* (line 11) indicates time or chronology of events.
- *And* (lines 24, 30, 37, 53, 54, 58) indicates additional information.
- *In fact* (line 28) indicates emphasis.
- *First of all* (line 48) indicates an example.
- *For instance* (line 49) indicates an example.
- *In addition* (line 55) indicates additional information.
- *First* (line 60) indicates an example.
- *Second* (line 62) indicates an example.

Post-Reading Activities

A. Comprehension Check

1. F   2. F   3. T   4. X   5. T   6. F
7. T   8. T   9. X

B. Vocabulary Check

1. Answers may vary. Foreign foods mentioned in the reading include: *black currant milk shakes, salads with shrimp, vegetarian burgers, tatsuta chicken sandwiches, McLaks salmon sandwiches.* You do not have to know exactly what these foods are because the main point is clear: McDonald's changes its menu to fit with different countries' foods. The specific foods listed are just examples of the main point.

2. Answers for some categories, such as "Can I use world knowledge?" will vary. Some sections of the chart may be completed as follows:

Word	Is it important?	Is there an internal definition?	It is a noun? verb? adjective?
1. cultures	Yes (The word repeats and appears in topic sentences.)	No	Noun
2. giant	No (It's a description word.)	No	Noun (also an adjective)
3. abroad	Yes (The word repeats.)	Yes (lines 11–12) *in other countries*	Noun
4. Belorussians	No (This is the specific name of a nationality.)	No	Noun
5. overlooks	Yes (The word is only used once, but it's important for understanding the example that supports the paragraph's main idea.)	No	Verb
6. Tiananmen	No (This is a specific place name.)	No	No
7. adapted	Yes (The word relates to the main idea of a paragraph.)	No	Verb
8. pleased	Yes (The word appears in a topic sentence.)	No	Adjective
9. Americanized	Yes (The word repeats in other forms, and the word appears in the conclusion paragraph of a letter.)	No	Verb
10. cleanliness	Yes (Although it's an item listed in a series, the word helps provide support for the paragraph's main idea.)	No	Noun
11. atmosphere	Yes (Although it's an item listed in a series, the word helps provide support for the paragraph's main idea.)	No	Noun

Choices of additional important unfamiliar words will vary. Possible unfamiliar, important words: *taking over, bullets, innocent, corporations, disappearing, factors, contributing, refuse.*

C. Following Ideas

The reference chart should be completed as follows:

Word	Line	Refers to
1. our cultures	2	X (no clear referent; no specific cultures or people are referred to)
2. they	11	McDonald's
3. there	12	X (no referent; subject of the sentence)
4. its	28	McDonald's
5. this amount	30	59 percent of its (McDonald's) profits
6. one	63	X (no referent; part of the subject of the sentence)

D. Predicting Ideas with Signal Words

The sentences should be ordered as follows with the signal words (in boldface here) identified:

1. There are many reasons for the success of fast-food chains like McDonald's.
2. **First of all**, they have adapted to foreign tastes.
3. **For instance**, McDonald's sells wine in France, black currant milk shakes in Poland, salads with shrimp in Germany, vegetarian burgers in the Netherlands and India, tatsuta chicken sandwiches (with ginger and soy sauce) in Japan, and a salmon sandwich called McLaks in Norway.
4. **In addition**, other factors contributing to fast-food success abroad are cleanliness, a family atmosphere, air conditioning, and efficient service.

E. Identifying Main Ideas

The main idea of each paragraph should be identified as follows:

Paragraph 1: People around the world may not know it, but our cultures are in danger.

Paragraph 2: The facts speak for themselves.

Paragraph 3: Think of all the money that American corporations are making from other countries.

Paragraph 4: In my opinion, American businesses like McDonald's are destroying our cultures.

Paragraph 7: It's ridiculous to say that American fast food is destroying other cultures.

Discuss
Student Book p. 108

Answers will vary.

Remember
Student Book p. 108

Charts may vary. A flow chart and a block diagram would both be possible. Possible flow chart of paragraph 4:

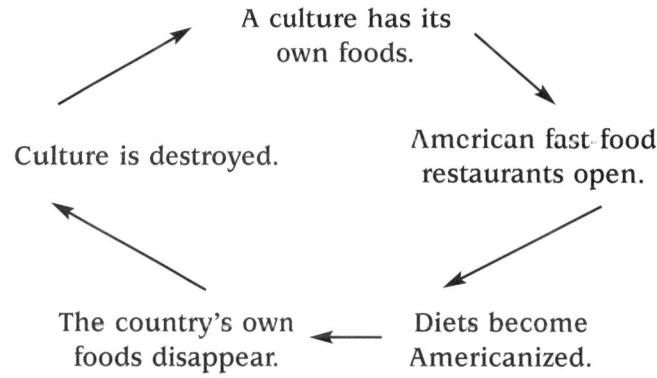

Reading: Underground World

Getting Started
Student Book p. 110

Answers will vary. Possible answer:

1. The underground world is the world beneath the earth's surface, a world of caves.

Prepare
Student Book p. 111

Answers may vary. Possible answers:

1. The reading is from a geology textbook. It is probably written for students (adult or teenage learners). The readers may have a special interest in caves or in earth sciences, or they may not.

2. The text will probably not be that difficult to read. Because it is from a textbook, the reading will be instructional. Important terms, which appear in italics, are defined. The labeled illustration also helps readers to understand key terms and concepts.

3. Possible terms related to *caves*: *wide, narrow, tunnel, shaft, mine, geology, rocks, lava, volcanic, explore, hide.*

4. Pre-reading questions will vary. Possible questions:
   - In what kinds of rock/material can caves be found?
   - How are caves formed?

Read
Student Book p. 111

Answers to the possible prediction questions from the *Prepare* section:

- Caves can be found in limestone, volcanic lava, and granite.

- Caves can be formed in different ways: water making cracks through limestone, volcanic activity forming caves in lava, ocean waves wearing away granite, and gases from oil fields carving out caves in limestone.

Read Again
Student Book p. 112

Practice of individual reading strategies should be encouraged; answers will vary.

Possible additional questions and answers:

> Question: Where can caves be found?
>
> Answer: Caves can be found in many places where the conditions are good for making caves, including Hawaii, Iceland, and New Mexico.
>
> Question: How long have caves been around?
>
> Answer: Caves have been around at least since the Stone Age.

The main idea of each paragraph should be identified as follows:

> Paragraph 1: Caves are fascinating places because no cave is exactly like another.
>
> Paragraph 2: People have been interested in caves since prehistoric times.
>
> Paragraph 3: Most caves are found in limestone rock.
>
> Paragraph 4: A small number of caves are found in other kinds of rock.

For connectors and referents, see *C. Following Ideas* on TM page 58.

Post-Reading Activities

A. Comprehension Check

1. Most caves 2. Most caves 3. Some caves
4. Some caves 5. Most caves 6. Some caves
7. Some caves 8. No caves 9. Some caves

B. Vocabulary Check

1. a. limestone b. lava c. granite

   You do not need to know exactly what types of rocks these are because it is clear in the reading how the caves are formed.

2. Answers for some categories, such as "Can I use world knowledge?" will vary. Some sections of the chart may be completed as follows:

Word or Phrase	Is it important?	Is there an internal definition?	It is a noun? verb? adjective?
1. multicolored	Yes (It's a description word, but it provides support for the topic sentence.)	No	Adjective
2. columns	Yes (The word repeats and helps provide support for the topic sentence.)	Yes (lines 4–5) Useful information: They are things that *come up from the floor* and *hang down from the ceiling*	Noun
3. stalagmites	Yes (The word repeats and is used in the illustration.)	Yes (line 4) *columns that come up from the floor*; also shown in the illustration	Noun
4. stalactites	Yes (The word repeats and is used in the illustration.)	Yes (lines 4–5) *columns that hang from the ceiling*; also shown in the illustration	Noun

Word or Phrase	Is it important?	Is there an internal definition?	It is a noun? verb? adjective?
5. prehistoric	Yes (The word is used in a topic sentence.)	Partially (line 6) Related term: *the Stone Age*	Noun
6. Stone Age	Yes (The word restates another word from the topic sentence, and provides support for the topic sentence.)	Partially (line 6) Related term: *prehistoric times*	Noun
7. spelunking	Yes (The word is defined.)	Yes (lines 7–8) *cave exploration is a sport*; (line 8) Synonyms: *caving, potholing*	Noun (It looks like a verb—it is an activity—but here it appears in a gerund form and functions as a noun.)
8. potholing	Yes (The word is defined.)	Yes (lines 7–8) *cave exploration is a sport*; (line 8) Synonyms: *spelunking, caving*	Noun (It looks like a verb. It is an activity, but here it appears in a gerund form and functions as a noun.)
9. speleology	Yes (The word is defined.)	Yes (line 9) *The scientific study of caves.*	Noun
10. cracks	Yes (The word repeats.)	No	Noun
11. dissolves	Yes (The word repeats in different forms.)	No	Verb
12. evaporates	Yes (The word explains an important step in a process.)	No (Although from context, it may be guessed in line 16 that the water goes into the air, disappears.)	Verb
13. erode	Yes (The word is defined.)	Yes (lines 22–23) Synonym: *wear away*	Verb

Choices of additional unfamiliar words will vary.
Possible unfamiliar, important words: *fascinating, exploration, oil fields.*

C. Following Ideas

The reference chart should be completed as follows:

Word or Phrase	Line	Refers to
1. it	8	cave exploration
2. it	12	water
3. this way	13	the process of water moving through cracks in the limestone, dissolving the rock.
4. this water	16	the water in a cave
5. they	24	gases from oil fields
6. The Big Room	24	X (subject of the sentence; no referent)

Remember
Student Book p. 114

Diagrams may vary. The diagram to show how a cave forms in limestone rock could be drawn as a horizontal flow chart or as a timeline.

| cracks form in limestone | water moves through cracks | water dissolves the limestone | cracks get larger and form large spaces | water evaporates, leaving limestone | water drips from roof, forming stalactites and stalagmites |

Discuss
Student Book p. 114

Answers will vary. Possible answers:

1. Other things that dissolve in water include paper, antacids, chalk.
2. Wind and rain can erode soil and rock. So can human activity (hiking, mountain biking, construction activities).

Prepare
Student Book p. 115

Answers may vary. Possible answers:

1. This reading will probably give mostly facts and descriptions. The subtitles indicate that facts will be given about each topic, and the illustrations indicate that clothing and equipment might be described.

2. The purpose of the text is probably to inform people about what they will need in order to go caving safely and comfortably. The article will probably be read by people who are interested in trying this sport. It will probably not be read by experts in the field.

3. Possible terms related to *caving* and *equipment*: *lights, shovel, ropes, helmet, kneepads, shoes, boots, gloves, rocks, injuries, emergencies.*

4. Pre-reading questions will vary. Possible questions:
   - What are the most important things to have if you want to go caving?
   - Why do you need special clothes to go caving?
   - Where can you buy clothing and equipment for caving?

Read
Student Book p. 115

Answers to the possible prediction questions from the *Prepare* section:

- The most important things to have for caving are a light and a helmet.
- Caving can destroy ordinary clothes. Special clothing can also offer protection to the knees, head, hands, and other body parts.
- You can buy most things for caving at stores that specialize in sports or outdoor activities (such as The Outdoor Store). Some things can also be purchased cheaply in a hardware store.

Read Again
Student Book p. 116

Practice of individual reading strategies should be encouraged; answers will vary.

Possible additional questions and answers:

Question: Why do you need a light and a helmet?

Answer: You need a light because caves are absolutely dark. You need a helmet because rocks often fall in caves.

Question: Why do you need special clothes?

Answer: Because caves destroy ordinary clothes.

The main reason why each piece of equipment is important:

- Light is important because caves are absolutely dark.
- Helmets are important because rocks often fall in caves, and the head should be protected.
- Clothing is important because caves can destroy ordinary clothes.
- Boots are important because caves can be wet.
- A backpack is important because you should bring food, water, and emergency supplies.

For connectors and referents, see *C. Following Ideas* on TM page 61.

For signal words and predictions, see *D. Predicting Ideas with Signal Words* on TM page 62.

Post-Reading Activities

A. Comprehension Check

1. two kinds of lights cavers use: electric lights, carbide lamps
2. the kind of energy each light uses: electricity, acetylene
3. cost of a helmet: $25.00
4. two kinds of boots cavers wear: army boots, jungle boots
5. why kneepads are important: caves can have low ceilings—you might need to crawl on your knees

60 CHAPTER 7

B. Vocabulary Check

1. *Ceiling* should be circled; it is the only word that is not clothing or an accessory for caving.

2. Answers for some categories, such as "Can I use world knowledge?" will vary. Some sections of the chart may be completed as follows:

Word	Is it important?	Is there an internal definition?	It is a noun? verb? adjective?
1. mandatory	Yes (It appears in the subtitle.)	Yes (line 1) Restatement: *you must carry with you*; (lines 13 and 16) Synonym: *necessary*	Adjective
2. absolutely	Yes (It appears in the first sentence of the article, topic sentence of the paragraph.)	No	Adverb
3. caving	Yes (It appears in the title, subtitle, and conclusion.)	No	Noun (It looks like a verb. It is an activity, but here it appears in a gerund form and functions as a noun.)
4. equipment	Yes (The word appears in the title and subtitle, as well as the conclusion.)	Yes (throughout article) Subheadings, examples, context: *lights, helmets, clothing, accessories*	Noun
5. traditional	No (It's a description word.)	No	Adjective
6. acetylene gas	No (It's a description of an item, and not really necessary for understanding the main idea of the paragraph.)	No	Noun
7. ordinary	Yes (The word appears in a topic sentence and helps to introduce the main idea of the paragraph.)	No	Adjective
8. army	No (The word repeats, but it's a descriptive word, part of the name of a specific kind of boot.)	No	Noun or adjective

Word	Is it important?	Is there an internal definition?	It is a noun? verb? adjective?
9. jungle	No (The word repeats, but it's a descriptive word, part of the name of a specific kind of boot.)	No	Noun or adjective
10. waterproof	Yes (The word is defined, and relates to the main idea of the paragraph.)	Yes (lines 23–24) *no water can get in*	Adjective
11. drain	Yes (The word relates to the main idea of the paragraph.)	Yes (line 24) *holes around the bottom*; (line 28) *allow the water to drain*	Verb (Though it's more commonly seen as a noun, it's a verb in an infinitive form here.)
12. gardening	No (It's a descriptive word, part of the name of a specific kind of glove.)	No	Adjective (Here, it describes the type of glove; often the word is seen as a verb or a gerund form of a noun.)
13. ceilings	Yes (The word appears in a topic sentence.)	No	Noun

Choices of additional unfamiliar words will vary. Possible unfamiliar, important words: *zoom, headlight, coveralls, hardware stores, sporting goods stores, hiking, daypack, battery, club.*

C. Following Ideas

The reference chart should be completed as follows:

Word or Phrase	Line	Refers to
1. this unit	5	the light on the left in the picture (or: the Zoom Headlight).
2. there	15	X (subject of the sentence; no referent)
3. it's	18	X (subject of the sentence; no referent)
4. that	20	a flight suit made by Franconia

Word or Phrase	Line	Refers to
5. this	26	water gets in at the top (of the boots)
6. they	28	jungle boots
7. that	42	X (subject of the sentence; no referent)
8. there	46	a caving club in your area

D. Predicting Ideas with Signal Words

1. Signal words and predictions:
   - *So* (lines 1, 13) indicates a result.
   - *And* (lines 3, 31, 39) indicates additional information.
   - *But* (lines 16, 27, 42) indicates contrasting information.
   - *Therefore* (line 18) indicates a result.
   - *Another* (line 21) indicates additional information.
   - *Also* (line 37) indicates additional information.
   - *Before* (line 43) indicates time or chronology of events.

2. Answers will vary.

Remember

Student Book p. 118

The chart can be completed as follows:

Equipment	Purpose	Cost
electric light	helps you see inside a cave	$40.00
carbide lamp	helps you see inside a cave	$50.00
flight suit	protects your clothing	$40.00
boots (army or jungle)	protect your feet and keep them dry	$35.00
gloves (leather and canvas gardening gloves)	protect your hands	$4.00
kneepads	protect your knees in caves with low ceilings	may depend on the style and quality and on where you buy them

Discuss
Student Book p. 118

1. Answers will vary.
2. Answers will vary. Possible answers: Many sports are not too expensive for ordinary people to do. It depends on the sport. Many sports, such as running, walking, or swimming, require little or no special equipment. Other sports, such as tennis, bicycling, or certain team sports, may require equipment, but people do not need to purchase the newest, most expensive equipment out there; many things can be purchased used or discounted. Some sports, such as skiing or hang-gliding, may be too expensive for some people to do; for these sports, the correct equipment may be necessary for safety reasons.

Prepare
Student Book p. 119

Answers may vary. Possible answers:

1. The title is about saving caves—possibly from some kind of destruction caused by nature or by humans.
2. Possible things that destroy caves: Natural causes—storms, wind, rain, heavy snows. Human causes—construction near or on top of caves, vandalism (spray painting walls, leaving garbage, starting fires), too many explorers walking through them.
3. Pre-reading questions will vary. Possible questions:
   - How can caves be damaged or destroyed?
   - How can caves be saved?

Read
Student Book p. 119

Answers to the possible prediction questions from the *Prepare* section:
- Caves can be damaged or destroyed by vandalism, visitors' touching the fragile stalagmites and stalactites, light, dry air, and changes in the humidity.
- Caves can be saved by developing them for responsible tourism. Visitors can be asked not to touch fragile stalagmites and stalactites. The amount of light can be controlled with computers. Dry air and humidity changes can be controlled with special doors.

Read Again
Student Book p. 120

Practice of individual reading strategies should be encouraged; answers will vary.

Possible additional questions and answers:

Question: Why do we need to protect caves?
Answer: Because people can easily destroy them through vandalism.

Question: How old is the cave in the article?
Answer: It is a "live" cave with formations that have been growing for tens of thousands of years.

The main idea of each paragraph should be identified as follows:

Paragraph 1: In November 1974, two young cavers, Gary Tenen and Randy Tufts, were exploring the limestone hills in the Whetstone Mountains in Arizona. There they found a small hole in the hillside.

Paragraph 2: For a long time, Tenen and Tufts told only a few people about the cave.

Paragraph 3: "Our whole purpose since day one has been to protect the cave," says Mr. Tufts.

Paragraph 4: State officials and speleologists have worked hard to protect the cave.

Paragraph 5: Caves can be destroyed in a number of other ways.

For connectors and referents, see *C. Following Ideas* on TM page 66

For signal words and predictions, see *D. Predicting Ideas with Signal Words* on TM page 66.

Post-Reading Activities

A. Comprehension Check

1. 1974 was the year that Gary Tenen and Randy Tufts discovered the Big Room. 1978 was the year that Tenen and Tufts told the property owners about the cave. 1988 was the year that the cave's existence was announced to the public, and the state of Arizona bought the cave to make a park.

2. The two young men kept the cave a secret because if people knew about the cave, they might destroy it.

3. Now, anyone in the general public can visit the cave.

4. Touching the stalagmites and stalactites can break them. Light can dry out a cave and cause algae to grow, which then destroys the beautiful colors in the rocks. Dry air and changes in the humidity can stop stalagmites and stalactites from growing.

5. The Kartchner Cave isn't called the "Tenen and Tufts Cave" because it was named after the people who owned the property the cave was on.

B. Vocabulary Check

1. A synonym for *cave* is *cavern* (line 8).

2. Two words related to *vandal* are *vandalized* (line 20) and *vandalism* (line 34). *Vandalized* is a past tense form of the verb *vandalize,* meaning to cause destruction to something (intentionally). *Vandalism* is a noun, meaning the act of destroying something (by spray painting, leaving garbage, etc.). The suffixes determine the word form and the meaning.

3. Answers for some categories, such as "Can I use world knowledge?" will vary. Some sections of the chart may be completed as follows:

Word	Is it important?	Is there an internal definition?	It is a noun? verb? adjective?
1. through	No (The word does not repeat or relate to a main idea, and it is clear from the rest of the sentence what is happening.)	No	None—preposition
2. moist	No (It is a description word, it does not repeat, and although it is useful to know that caves are moist, it is not essential for understanding the paragraph.)	No (Although in lines 42–43, a contrasting word, *dry air*, is given and we learn that dry air can destroy caves.)	Adjective
3. enlarge	No (The word does not repeat or relate to a main idea, and it is clear from the rest of the sentence what is happening.)	No	Verb

Word	Is it important?	Is there an internal definition?	It is a noun? verb? adjective?
4. squeeze	No (The word does not repeat or relate to a main idea, and it is clear from the rest of the sentence what is happening.)	No	Verb
5. historically	Yes (It relates to the main point of the paragraph—time/history has shown that vandalism occurs in caves.)	No	Adverb
6. vandalized	Yes (The word repeats in different forms.)	Yes (line 21) Examples: *spray paint on walls, break the formations, leave trash*	Verb
7. trash	Yes (The word is part of a definition of a key word.)	No	Noun
8. existence	Yes (The word appears in a topic sentence.)	No	Noun
9. fragile	Yes (The word is a description word, but it is part of a supporting point related to a main idea.)	No	Adjective
10. algae	Yes (The word repeats.)	No	Noun

Choices of additional unfamiliar words will vary. Possible unfamiliar, important words: *cavers, owners, terribly, protect, announced, measures.*

66 CHAPTER 7

C. Following Ideas

The reference chart should be completed as follows:

Word or Phrase	Line	Refers to
1. there	3	the limestone hills in the Whetstone Mountains in Arizona
2. the young men	14–15	Tenen and Tufts
3. this	20	the cave (that the boys found)/The Big Room
4. that	23	vandalized terribly by people who spray paint on walls, break the formations, leave trash. (OR destroy a cave)
5. this	29	state officials and speleologists have worked hard to protect the cave
6. they	32	state officials and speleologists
7. it	39	a cave
8. these measures	47–48	visitors are not allowed to touch them; computers control the lights in the Kartchner caves; the Kartchner caves are protected by special doors

D. Predicting Ideas with Signal Words

Predictions may vary. Answers are as follows:

a. after = (line 6) Information that comes before it is an event: Tenen and Tufts dig a hole into the hillside and enlarge it. *After* indicates chronology.

b. for example = (lines 35–36) Information that comes before it is general: caves can be destroyed in other ways besides vandalism. *For example* indicates an example for the general information.

c. in addition = (lines 37–38) Information that comes before it gives an example: The stalactites and stalagmites are extremely fragile, so visitors aren't allowed to touch them. *In addition* indicates an additional example.

d. therefore = (line 41) Information that comes before it explains a condition: Heat from lights can dry out the cave and allow algae to grow; algae destroys the colors in the rocks. *Therefore* indicates the result of the condition.

E. Identifying the Main Idea

Answers may vary. Possible answers:

Part 1
Main idea: The discovery of the Kartchner Cave
Subtitle: How the Big Room/the Kartchner Cave was Discovered

Part 2
Main idea: The preservation and protection of the Kartchner Cave
Subtitle: Protecting the Kartchner Cave

CHAPTER 7   **67**

Remember
Student Book p. 122

The chart can be completed as follows:

How Can You Keep a Cave Alive?	
Problem	Solution
1. vandalism (People spray paint on walls, break the rock formations, leave trash.)	Control how many people can visit the cave, and at what times; provide rules about what can be done, what can be touched, and where people can go.
2. light (The heat from light can dry out a cave, and light allows algae to grow; algae then destroys the beautiful colors of the rocks.)	Control the light with computers.
3. dry air/changes in the humidity (Dry air from outside can destroy a cave, and even small changes in the humidity can stop stalagmites and stalactites from growing.)	Use special doors to keep the humidity at 98% at all times and to prevent dry air from coming in.

Discuss
Student Book p. 122

Answers will vary. Possible answers:

1. Yes, governments should spend money to save a cave. Caves are natural wonders. People should be encouraged to visit caves and to learn about and respect the environment. People will care more about the environment if they have opportunities to appreciate nature. **(OR)** No, governments should not spend money to save a cave. Caves can be saved with private funding. There are plenty of special interest groups that can raise money to save caves, or private donations can be used. Government money should be used for resources that help people, such as schools and housing. There isn't enough money to spend on something that is underground and that people don't use every day.

READING 4

Prepare
Student Book p. 123

Answers may vary. Possible answers:

1. The title and the photo suggest that the topic is an attraction somewhere, a history of an underground garden, which was probably one person's dream to create.

2. Other features of the reading include admission information (prices) and contact information for reservations. This suggests that the reading is from a brochure or a travel guide.

3. The text will probably not answer the question "How many people see the gardens every year?" The reason is that, according to the subtitle, the article is primarily a history of the place. It is probably more about the past than about how many people go there today.

68 CHAPTER 7

Possible additional questions:

- Where are the underground gardens located?
- Is this place open to the public or to tourists? If so, when?

Read
Student Book p. 123

Answers to the possible additional prediction questions from the *Prepare* section:

- The Forestiere Underground Gardens are located in Fresno, California.
- The place is open to tourists, from Wednesday through Sunday, 10 A.M. to 4 P.M. Tours require an advance reservation.

Read Again
Student Book p. 124

Practice of individual reading strategies should be encouraged; answers will vary.

Possible additional questions and answers:

Question: Who was the man who had the "dream" of these gardens? (Who created the gardens?)

Answer: The man who created these gardens was Baldasare Forestiere, an immigrant from Sicily, who dreamed of growing a garden but found that the dirt on his land was not usable.

Question: How big are the Underground Gardens?

Answer: The gardens are beneath 10 acres of land. They include more than 50 rooms and 100 patios and courtyards.

The reading could be divided into two parts as follows:

Part 1
Main idea: The History of the Underground Gardens (lines 1–15)

Part 2
Main idea: Visiting the Underground Gardens (lines 16–end)

For connectors and referents, see *C. Following Ideas* on TM page 71.

Signal words and predictions:

- *In (year)* (line 1) indicates time or chronology of events.
- *And* (lines 4, 10, 11, 13, 17–20, 25, 36, 42) indicates additional information.
- *However* (line 7) indicates contrasting information.
- *So* (line 8) indicates a result.
- *Also* (line 23) indicates additional information.
- *After* (line 31) indicates time or chronology of events.

Post-Reading Activities

A. Comprehension Check

1. The man who created these gardens was Baldasare Forestiere, an immigrant from Sicily, who dreamed of growing a garden but found that the dirt on his land was not usable.
2. The Underground Gardens are in Fresno, California.
3. Baldasare built them by digging underground, using only hand tools.
4. The gardens have more than 50 rooms.
5. The plants in the Underground Gardens include fruit trees and grapevines.
6. Yes, Baldasare lived underground. He built beds into the walls and carved a bathtub into the rock.
7. Museum admission costs $6.00 for adults, $5.00 for seniors and students, and $3.00 for children over five. Children under five are admitted for free.
8. You can contact the museum by calling them at the number provided: (559) 555-0734. You could also write to them at the address provided.

B. Vocabulary Check

Answers for some categories, such as "Can I use world knowledge?" will vary. Some sections of the chart may be completed as follows:

Word	Is it important?	Is there an internal definition?	It is a noun? verb? adjective?
1. hardpan	Yes (The word appears in the introduction, and relates to the main idea of the article.)	Yes (lines 5–6) *hard dirt, that is completely useless for agriculture*	Noun
2. agriculture	Yes (The word appears in the introduction, and relates to the main idea of the article.)	No (But the context in lines 3-4 helps define the word: *He dreamed of growing trees and vines.*)	Noun
3. unwilling	Yes (It appears in a topic sentence.)	No (But the context of the sentence helps to define the word; contrasting information is given in the next clause: *he was unwilling to give up his dream, so he began to dig.*)	Adjective
4. carved out	Yes (It relates to the main idea of the paragraph and of the article, and the word repeats.)	Yes (line 8) Synonym: *dig*	Verb
5. wonderland	Yes (It relates to the main idea of the paragraph and of the article.)	No	Noun
6. courtyards	Yes (It's an item in a list, but the word repeats and it directly relates to the main idea; it helps to describe the gardens.)	Yes (line 18) Explanation of what they do: *let in sunlight and rainwater*	Noun
7. patios	Yes (It's an item in a list, and the word does not repeat, but it directly relates to the main idea; it helps to describe the gardens.)	No	Noun

Word	Is it important?	Is there an internal definition?	It is a noun? verb? adjective?
8. beneath	Yes (Similar/related words appear in the reading.)	Yes (line 9 and elsewhere) Related word: *underground*; (line 21) Related word: *below*	Preposition
9. acres	No (It's not important to know the exact unit of measurement, only to recognize that it's a large area.)	No	Noun
10. skylights	Yes (The word does not repeat, but it directly relates to the main idea; it helps to describe the gardens.)	Yes (lines 17–18) Explanation of what they do: *let in sunlight and rainwater*	Noun
11. frost	No (The word does not repeat, and the main idea of the paragraph can be understood without an exact definition—it is enough to recognize that it is something cold.)	Yes (lines 20–21) Contrasting word/idea: *the heat above and the frost below*	Noun
12. emerge	Yes (The word does not repeat, but it directly relates to the main idea; it helps to describe the gardens.)	No (But the context in line 21 helps define the word: *above the ground*.)	Verb
13. tunnels	Yes (The word does not repeat, but it directly relates to the main idea; it helps to describe the gardens.)	Yes (line 10) Synonym: *passageways*; (Also the context in lines 25–26 helps define the word: *that go from one end to another.*)	Noun

Choices of additional unfamiliar words may vary.
Possible unfamiliar, important words: *vines, passageways, amazingly, hand tools, awesome, bushes, dreamer, museum, advance reservation.*

C. Following Ideas

The reference chart should be completed as follows:

Word or Phrase	Line	Refers to
1. there	2	Fresno, California
2. them	20	the fruit trees and grapevines
3. all of this	26	the Underground Gardens or, more specifically, the beds built into the walls, the bathtub carved into the rock, and long tunnels that go from one end to another
4. that	28-29	to make something with lots of money
5. that	29-30	to make something out of nothing

Remember
Student Book p. 126

Answers may vary. Possible answers:

What? The Underground Gardens
Where? Fresno, California
When? Started in 1905, when Baldasare Forestiere bought his land. Today it's a museum open to the public on certain days of the week, at certain hours.
Why?   He dreamed of growing trees and vines, but his land was hardpan and he could grow nothing on top of it.
How?   Dug into the ground, with hand tools
Who?   Baldasare Forestiere

Cluster diagrams will vary.

Discuss
Student Book p. 126

Answers will vary.

CHAPTER 8
Reading: Numbers, Numbers, Numbers

Getting Started
Student Book p. 128

1. Answers will vary.
2. Answers may vary. Possible ways that people figure numbers and amounts: fingers, calculators, adding machines, and abacus; add, subtract, multiply, divide.
3. Answers may vary. Possible answer: The titles of the readings and the illustrations suggest that this chapter will have readings related to math and numbers. The readings may be

about the history of numbers (or of performing certain types of calculations), how other cultures consider numbers, and how some mathematical formulas work.

Prepare
Student Book p. 129

Answers will vary. Possible answers:

1. *Sense* means perception, recognition, or understanding of something.
2. The genre is probably a magazine article. It seems to be written for a general audience of adult and possibly teen readers. The purpose may be to inform readers about different ways of understanding numbers, or how people and animals understand numbers. The article does not use subtitles/headings, complex terms, or illustrations. The sentences do not seem very long. The author is not named. The reading does not seem very difficult.
3. Answers will vary.
4. Pre-reading questions will vary. Possible wh-questions:
   - How well do animals understand numbers?
   - What is number sense?

Read
Student Book p. 129

Answers to the possible prediction questions from the *Prepare* section:
- Some animals, such as birds and wasps, can recognize changes in numbers. However, some animals do this better than others.
- Number sense is the ability to recognize changes in numbers (not to count).

Read Again
Student Book p. 130

Practice of individual reading strategies should be encouraged; answers will vary.

Possible additional questions and answers:

Question: How well do humans understand numbers?

Answer: Humans are born with an ability to recognize number changes. However, when they are young, humans do not have a very good understanding of number changes; their understanding is almost as good as a crow's, and they are easily fooled.

Question: Which animals have some understanding of numbers?

Answer: Birds and wasps can understand number changes.

Students should note that the main ideas for each paragraph are located in topic sentences (the first sentence of each paragraph) and that specific examples follow.

For connectors and referents, see *C. Following Ideas* on TM page 74.

Signal words and predictions:
- *For instance* (line 3) indicates an example.
- *And* (lines 3, 5, 9-11, 14-16) indicates additional information.
- *However* (line 4) indicates contrasting information.
- *Another* (line 6) indicates additional information.
- *But* (lines 7, 9, 19) indicates contrasting information.
- *For example* (line 18) indicates an example.
- *Although* (line 21) indicates contrasting information.

Post-Reading Activities

A. Comprehension Check
1. F   2. F   3. T   4. F   5. F   6. F

B. Vocabulary Check
Answers for some categories, such as "Can I use world knowledge?" will vary. Some sections of the chart may be completed as follows:

Word	Is it important?	Is there an internal definition?	It is a noun? verb? adjective?
1. number sense	Yes (It appears in the title and topic sentences; it repeats; it is the subject of the reading.)	Yes (line 1) *Number sense is not the ability to count. It is the ability to recognize a change in number.*	Noun (compound noun)
2. recognize	Yes (The word is part of a definition of another key term, and there are repeated synonyms.)	Yes (line 4 and elsewhere) Synonym: *notice*	Verb
3. notice	Yes (The word repeats.)	Yes (line 1) Synonym: *recognize*	Verb
4. incredible	Yes (It's a description word, but the word appears in a topic sentence.)	No (But from the context, we can understand that it is a positive word, similar to *amazing*.)	Adjective
5. crow	Yes (The word repeats, and is the subject of an example that supports a main idea.)	No (We can tell from the context that is a type of bird, but we don't learn anything more specific.)	Noun
6. tower	Yes (The word repeats.)	No	Noun
7. fool	Yes (The word repeats.)	No (But we can tell from the context that it is a contrasting idea to *recognize/notice*.)	Verb
8. wasps	Yes (It appears in a topic sentence, and it is the subject of an example that supports a main idea.)	No (We know from the context that wasps are a type of insect, but we don't learn anything more specific.)	Noun

74 CHAPTER 8

Word	Is it important?	Is there an internal definition?	It is a noun? verb? adjective?
9. lays	Yes (It is important for understanding the main idea of the paragraph.)	No (But from context, we can tell that it means *leaving* eggs.)	Verb
10. cells	Yes (The word repeats.)	No	Noun
11. caterpillars	Yes (The word repeats and is important for understanding the example.)	No (But we can tell from the context that it is something that baby wasps could eat.)	Noun

Choices of additional unfamiliar words will vary. Possible unfamiliar, importatnt words: *ability, surprisingly, remove, generally, demonstrated, nest, insect.*

C. Following Ideas

The reference chart should be completed as follows:

Word or Phrase	Line	Refers to
1. this ability	2	the ability to recognize a change in number
2. this	4	If a nest has four eggs and you remove one, the bird will not notice. However, if you remove two, the bird generally leaves.
3. she	7	the crow
4. the other	9	man (or "another man")
5. it	11	X (subject of the sentence; no referent)
6. her	13	the female wasp
7. the children	20	babies about 14 months old

D. Predicting Ideas with Signal Words

The paragraph should be rewritten with the sentences in the following order:

> For instance, many birds have good number sense. If a nest has four eggs and you remove one, the bird will not notice. However, if you remove two, the bird generally leaves. This means that the bird knows the difference between two and three.

E. Identifying the Main Idea

The examples prove the following points:

1. eggs in the nest: proves the point that many birds have good number sense
2. the crow: proves the point that a bird has incredible number sense
3. the wasps: proves the point that in the insect world, wasps seem to have the best number sense
4. 14-month old children: proves the point that a human's number sense is not very good

Remember
Student Book p. 132

Graphic organizers may vary. The most logical graphic organizer to use to illustrate the idea of paragraph 4 is a cluster diagram. This is because the process of wasps laying their eggs is not the focus of the paragraph; a timeline, block diagram, or flow chart would not work well here. The focus of the paragraph is on the variations.

Students might write "Female wasps" in the center of the cluster diagram and branch off from there with specific information. "Lay eggs in individual cells" and "leave caterpillars for their young" could branch off from "Female wasps." Information about how many caterpillars are left ("5," "12," "24," "5 in a male cell," "10 in a female cell") could branch off from "leave caterpillars for their young."

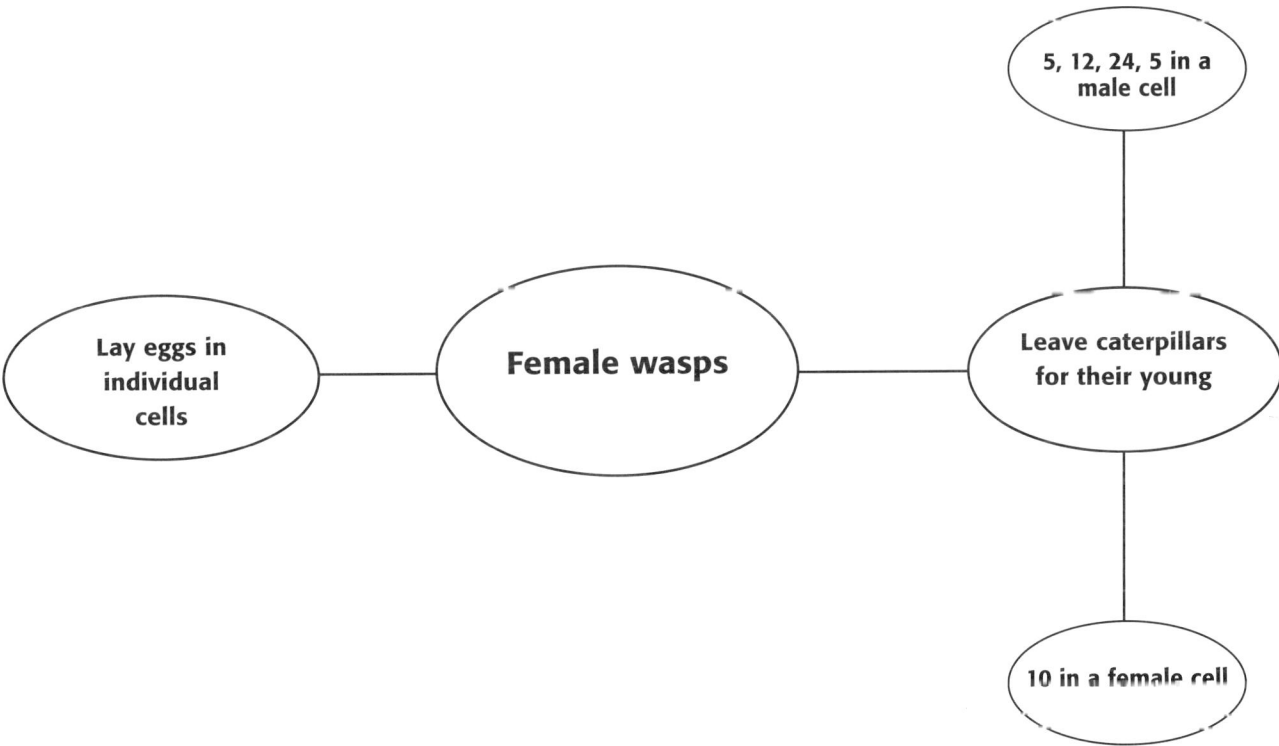

Discuss
Student Book p. 132

1. Answers will vary. Possible answer: Number sense helps animals know if they are missing one of their babies. It may also help animals recognize changes in their living environment/surroundings.

2. Answers will vary. Possible answers: Some animals may be as intelligent as or even more intelligent than humans. There is a lot that researchers still have to learn about animals. Some animals, like gorillas and orangutans, actually communicate through sign language, and they display behaviors toward their young that are similar to those of humans. We should not assume that all animals are unintelligent; we still have a lot to learn. **(OR)** Some animals are more intelligent than others. Researchers have done many kinds of experiments to test animal intelligence. Some animals can learn certain behaviors (for example, dogs can learn tricks, mice can learn to do tasks for a reward). However, animals mostly use instinct (automatic responses to things); they do not seem to think or be able to perform complex actions in the way that humans do.

Prepare
Student Book p. 133

Answers may vary. Possible answers:

76   CHAPTER 8

1. The reading has four parts. The topic of the reading is the abacus—what it looks like, how to use it, and different styles of it.
2. This reading could be from a textbook, a website, or a magazine article. It seems to be written for a general audience of adult and/or teen readers. It does not use much specialized vocabulary, and the sentences do not look long or complex. The illustration helps to show what an abacus is and how it works. The author and his/her position are not named. The purpose of the article seems to be to explain—to inform readers about the abacus. It does not look very difficult to read.
3. Possible terms related to the abacus: *calculate, calculator, count, add, subtract, beads, up, down, horizontal, vertical, difference, variations, ancient*.
4. Pre-reading questions will vary. Possible questions:
    - Where are (or were) abacuses used?
    - How do abacuses work?

Read
Student Book p. 133

Answers to the possible prediction questions from the *Prepare* section:
- Abacuses are used primarily in Asian countries such as China, Korea, and Japan. However, an ancient abacus has been found in Mexico, so people from other cultures used them as well.
- Abacuses work by moving beads; each bead represents a number value.

Read Again
Student Book p. 133

Practice of individual reading strategies should be encouraged; answers will vary.

Possible additional questions and answers:

Question: What are abacuses used for?
Answer: Abacuses are used for counting and for performing basic calculations (such as addition and subtraction).

Question: Are all abacuses the same?

Answer: No, there are different types of abacuses—the 2/5 (Chinese) abacus and the 1/4 (Japanese) abacus.

The main ideas of each section should be identified by the headings (subtitles).

Connectors and referents:
- *These* (line 5) refers to two sections of the abacus.
- *Each* (line 6) refers to the beads in the upper deck.
- *Each* (line 7) refers to the beads in the lower deck.
- *The next* (line 9) refers to the second rod from the far right.
- *The next* (line 10) refers to the third rod from the far right.
- *It* (line 11) refers to the third column from the left.
- *Each* (line 12) refers to the beads from the bottom deck.
- *It* (line 14) refers to the fourth column.
- *Five* (line 16) refers to beads.
- *This type* (line 16) refers to the Chinese abacus with two beads on the upper deck and five beads on the lower deck.
- *It* (line 17) refers to the most popular Japanese abacus.

Signal words and predictions:
- *And* (line 1, 3, 5, 12, 14, 16, 18) indicates additional information.
- *Next* (lines 9–10) indicates listing or order.
- *Similarly* (line 14) indicates an additional example.
- *Although* (line 19) indicates contrasting information.
- *For example* (line 20) indicates an example.

Note that *next* in this reading serves as both a connector and a signal word. It refers to the rods in the abacus and also helps the reader follow the description of the abacus rods from right to left.

Post-Reading Activities

A. Comprehension Check

1. F   2. F   3. T   4. F   5. T   6. F

B. Vocabulary Check

Answers for some categories, such as "Can I use world knowledge?" will vary. Some sections of the chart may be completed as follows:

Word	Is it important?	Is there an internal definition?	It is a noun? verb? adjective?
1. abacus	Yes (It is in the title, subtitles/headings, and topic sentences.)	Yes (line 1) *An abacus is a manual calculator that is common in China, Korea, and Japan.*	Noun
2. manual	Yes (It is part of the definition of a key word, and it is important to the main idea.)	No (But we may be able to tell from the context that it means *by hand*—the beads are moved by a person, not by anything else.)	Adjective
3. calculator	Yes (It is part of the definition of a key word, and it is important to the main idea.)	No (But we may be able to tell from the context that it is a thing used for counting and for performing other mathematical functions.)	Noun
4. frame	Yes (The word appears in a topic sentence and it repeats.)	No (However, it is labeled in the illustration.)	Noun
5. vertical	Yes (It appears in a topic sentence and is part of the description of the abacus.)	Yes (lines 3–4) *up and down*; (also line 4) Antonym: *horizontal*	Adjective
6. rod	Yes (It appears in a topic sentence and is part of the description of the abacus.)	No (However, it is labeled on the illustration.)	Noun
7. horizontal	Yes (It appears in a topic sentence, is part of the description of the abacus, and repeats.)	Yes (line 2) Antonym: *vertical*	Adjective
8. upper	Yes (The word repeats, is part of a description of the topic, and appears on an illustration.)	Yes (line 5) Antonym: *lower*	Adjective

Word	Is it important?	Is there an internal definition?	It is a noun? verb? adjective?
9. deck	Yes (The word repeats, is part of a description of the topic, and appears on an illustration.)	Yes (line 5) *sections*	Noun
10. bead	Yes (The word repeats, is part of a description of the topic, and appears on an illustration.)	No (But we learn in line 3 that the beads are *wooden* and moveable; also, they are labeled on an illustration.)	Noun
11. value	Yes (The word repeats and is directly related to the topic.)	Yes (throughout the reading) Numbers are given as examples of *values*; *values* are numbers.	Noun
12. represents	Yes (The word appears in a topic sentence.)	No (But from the context, we can guess that the word means *equals* or *stands for*.)	Verb
13. archaeologist	No (The word is used only once, and is not that important for understanding the main idea—the focus of the sentence is on the abacus that was found, not the type of person who found it.)	No	Noun

Choices of additional unfamiliar words will vary. Possible unfamiliar, important words: *totaling, sum, associated (with)*.

C. Identifying the Main Idea

1. An abacus is a manual calculator that is common in China, Korea, and Japan.
2. An abacus has a frame, several vertical rods, and beads. A horizontal piece separates the frame into two sections (or "decks").
3. Numbers are counted by moving beads toward the horizontal piece that separates the frame into two decks. The beads have different values.
4. Different types of abacuses are the Chinese 2/5 abacus and the Japanese 1/4 abacus.

Remember
Student Book p. 135

Illustrations may vary. Students should include and label the following parts: *frame, vertical rods, beads*. They may label the columns *ones* (on the far right), *tens, hundreds, thousands*, etc. If students have drawn a standard 2/5 or 1/4 abacus, they should show the number "57" as follows: on the far right rod (the "ones"), one bead from the upper deck and two beads from the lower deck and on the next rod (the "tens"), one bead from the upper deck.

CHAPTER 8   79

Discuss
Student Book p. 135

1. Answers will vary.
2. Answers will vary. Possible answers: No, it is not a good idea for banks and other businesses to continue to use the abacus. There is too much room for human error. In addition, the computer can make calculations much more quickly. The abacus no longer works in our modern, high-tech society. **(OR)** Yes, it is a good idea for banks and other businesses to use the abacus. Our society moves too quickly these days, and it is too dependent on technology like computers. Computers can always fail, or the power can go out, but the abacus will always work.

Prepare
Student Book p. 136

Answers may vary. Possible answers:

1. The topic of the reading may be about numbers and how they are written, about the history of zero, or about numbers that have no value.
2. The textbook may be a math book; it may also be a history book, with information about ancient Rome.
3. Possible terms related to Roman numerals and the topic: *I, II, III, IV, V, VI, VII, VIII, IX, X (etc.), calculate/calculations, add, subtract, multiply, divide, position, decimal, amounts.*
4. Pre-reading questions will vary. Possible questions:
   • Who invented "nothing"?
   • Why was "nothing" invented?

Read
Student Book p. 135

Answers to the possible prediction questions from the *Prepare* section:
   • "Nothing," or zero, was invented in India.
   • "Nothing," or zero, was invented as a symbol, or placeholder, to show number position and to simplify writing and calculating numbers. Before that, writing and calculating numbers was very complex.

Read Again
Student Book p. 137

Practice of individual reading strategies should be encouraged; answers will vary.

Possible additional questions and answers:
   Question: What happened before "nothing" was invented?
   Answer: Before "nothing" was invented, the Roman number system was used.
   Question: What number system do we use today?
   Answer: We use the Arabic number system, which has a zero.

Examples and key points should be identified; students can underline the topic sentence of each paragraph (preceding the examples) as follows:

   Paragraph 1: They (the Romans) never developed a number system that they could easily use for calculating.
   Paragraph 2: The Roman number system has seven symbols.
   Paragraph 3: In order to represent some numbers, they (the Romans) had to repeat symbols.
   Paragraph 4: The number system we use today is much simpler.
   Paragraph 5: With 0, a number system can use *position* to show amount.
   Paragraph 6: Using position makes the number system easier to understand in another important way: Longer numbers are bigger than shorter numbers.
   Paragraph 7: And look what happens when you try to multiply with Roman numerals.
   Paragraph 8: The zero was actually invented in India!

For connectors and referents, see *C. Following Ideas* on TM page 81.

For signal words and predictions, see *D. Predicting Ideas with Signal Words* on TM page 82.

Post-Reading Activities

A. Comprehension Check

The chart should be completed as follows:

	The Roman Number System	The Arabic Number System
1. has seven symbols	X	
2. has a zero		X
3. is good for counting and recording amounts	X	
4. is easy to use for calculations		X
5. uses position to show amounts		X
6. has nine symbols		X

B. Vocabulary Check

Answers for some categories, such as "Can I use world knowledge?" will vary. Some sections of the chart may be completed as follows:

Word	Is it important?	Is there an internal definition?	It is a noun? verb? adjective?
1. deficient	Yes (It's a description word, but it appears in the first line of the text.)	No (However, from context we can guess that it is a negative word, suggesting they weren't good at or didn't have something; lines 1–2: *They never developed a number system that they could easily use for calculating*.)	Adjective
2. calculating	Yes (The word repeats in different forms.)	No (However, from context we can guess that it has to do with addition, subtraction, and multiplication—mathematical functions which are mentioned in the reading.)	Noun (here, the word looks like a verb—it refers to an activity—but it is used as a gerund, a noun)

CHAPTER 8   **81**

Word	Is it important?	Is there an internal definition?	It is a noun? verb? adjective?
3. addition	Yes (The word repeats in different forms.)	No (However, we may be able to guess from context: it is a type of calculation, and it is presented in contrast to *counting and recording amounts*, line 3.)	Noun
4. symbol	Yes (The word repeats and is used in topic sentences.)	Yes (line 13–14) Examples: *5 (V), 50 (L)* and *500 (D)*; (also line 14) Internal definition: *represent some numbers*	Noun
5. position	Yes (The word repeats, is given in italics for emphasis, and appears in topic sentences.)	Yes (line 24) Synonym: *place*	Noun
6. digit	Yes (The word appears only once, but it is used in an explanation of an example related to the main idea.)	Yes (line 26) Synonym: *numbers*	Noun

Choices of additional unfamiliar words will vary. Possible unfamiliar, important words: *empire, recording, amounts, subtract, invent.*

C. Following Ideas

The reference chart should be completed as follows:

Word	Line	Refers to
1. they	1	the Romans
2. it	17	the Arabic number system we use today
3. there	24	X (subject of the sentence; no referent)
4. it	26	1,000
5. this	35	the Indians developed a symbol for nothing (zero).

D. Predicting Ideas with Signal Words

1. a. because (of) = line 18
   b. for instance = line 14
   c. however = lines 1, 3
   d. therefore = line 15

2. a. because (of) = since, so
   b. for instance = for example (students may note that this signal is also used in lines 18 and 26 of the reading); as an example; to illustrate
   c. however = but, in contrast, although, even though
   d. therefore = consequently, as a result

3. a. because = connects *the zero* as the cause with *using the same symbol again and again* as the result
   Possible restatement: Since our number system uses a 0, we can use the same symbol again and again. **(OR)** Our number system uses a 0, so we can use the same symbol again and again.

   b. for instance = connects an example (*3 was III, and 20 was XX*) to the more general preceding statement (*In order to represent some numbers, they had to repeat symbols.*)
   Possible restatement: In order to represent some numbers, they had to repeat symbols. To illustrate, 3 was III, and 20 was XX. **(OR)** In order to represent some numbers, they had to repeat symbols; for example, 3 was III, and 20 was XX.

   c. however = (line 1) connects the following two contrasting ideas: *We think of the Romans as having a great empire* and *In one area the Romans were deficient.*
   Possible restatement: We think of the Romans as having a great empire, but in one area they were deficient. **(OR)** Although we think of the Romans as having a great empire, in one area they were deficient.

   = (line 3) connects the following two contrasting ideas: *The system of Roman numerals was good for counting and recording amounts* and *Even simple addition was a slow process.*
   Possible restatement: The system of Roman numerals was good for counting and recording amounts, but even simple addition was a slow process. **(OR)** Even though the system of Roman numerals was good for counting and recording amounts, even simple addition was a slow process.

   d. therefore = connects the situation *To represent numbers, they had to add and subtract symbols* to the result or consequence *IV (1,5) represented 4, and VI (5,1) represented 6.*
   Possible restatement: To represent other numbers, they had to add and subtract symbols. Consequently, IV (1, 5) represented 4, and VI (5, 1) represented 6. **(OR)** To represent other numbers, they had to add and subtract symbols. As a result, IV (1, 5) represented 4, and VI (5, 1) represented 6.

Remember
Student Book p. 139

Graphic organizers may vary. The most logical graphic organizer to use to chart the disadvantages of the Roman number system is a cluster diagram, since this topic does not describe a process over time or a series of causes and effects. Students may write "Disadvantages of the Roman number system" in the center and branch off from there with different disadvantages:

- they had to repeat symbols to represent some numbers
- simple addition was a slow process
- no zero or place holder
- longer numbers are not necessarily bigger than shorter numbers
- multiplication is very complicated

Discuss
Student Book p. 139

1. Answers will vary. Possible answers: Roman numerals are still used today in many books (especially textbooks) to organize sections, units, chapters, etc. They can often be seen in the Table of Contents at the beginning of a book. Roman numerals are also commonly used in outlines (for things like formal reports, long research papers, and presentations).

2. Answers will vary. Possible answers: Other ancient peoples may have made simple marks (like tally marks) to indicate numbers, or they may have used other kinds of symbols (for

example, the ancient Egyptians used pictograms). Many ancient civilizations, such as the Mayans, used sophisticated number systems. If you lived in the Stone Age, you might have used a very simple number system.

Prepare
Student Book p. 139

1. b. an ancient people's number system
2. b. numbers, bars, and dots.
3. c. What was the number system of the Maya?

Read
Student Book p. 140

Answer to the possible prediction question from the *Prepare* section:

- The number system of the Maya was a system of symbols; bars and dots represented numbers, and position of numbers was shown vertically.

Read Again
Student Book p. 141

Practice of individual reading strategies should be encouraged; answers will vary.

Possible wh– questions and answers:

Question: How was the Mayan number system different from ours?

Answer: They used a base number of 20, rather than the 10 digits we use today. In addition, they used a system of bars and dots as symbols, and they showed number position vertically rather than horizontally.

Question: How did the Maya represent numbers?

Answer: They used the symbols of bars and dots. A bar represented 5; a dot represented 1.

Question: How did the Maya add numbers?

Answer: They lined up the numbers from bottom to top and then added up the bars and dots.

Examples and key points should be identified as follows:

Paragraph 3: 32 is 3 X 10 + 2 (in our decimal system) and 1 X 20 + 12 (in the Mayan system) are examples that illustrate the point *Because the base of the number system was 20, larger numbers were written down in powers of 20.*

Paragraph 4: Lines 18–21 and lines 23–24 give examples to illustrate the point *Instead of going from left to right, their numbers were written from bottom to top.*

Paragraph 5: Lines 27–29 give an example to illustrate *It was easy to add and subtract using this number system.*

For signal words and predictions, see *C. Predicting Ideas with Signal Words* on TM page 85.

Post-Reading Activities

A. Comprehension Check

The chart should be completed as follows:

	The Mayan Number System	The Arabic Number System
1. has two symbols	X	
2. has a zero (0)	X	X
3. is easy to use for counting	X	X
4. is easy to use for calculations	X	X

	The Mayan Number System	The Arabic Number System
5. uses position to show amounts	X	X
6. writes numbers from bottom to top	X	

B. Vocabulary Check

1. *Shorthand* means writing something in a short (abbreviated) version—using symbols rather than entire words or numbers. Shorthand is a noun.

2. A noun form of the verb *calculate* can be found in line 32: *calculations*. The suffix is *-tion*, indicating that it is a noun.

3. Answers for some categories, such as "Can I use world knowledge?" will vary. Some sections of the chart may be completed as follows:

Word	Is it important?	Is there an internal definition?	It is a noun? verb? adjective?
1. base	Yes (The word repeats and appears in topic sentences.)	No (However, from the illustration and the context we might guess the meaning.)	Noun
2. shorthand	Yes (The word is used to explain a main idea.)	No (However, from the context, we might guess that shorthand involves a system of representing something with symbols; the word *represented* is used right after it, line 5.)	Noun
3. powers	Yes (The word is part of an explanation directly related to the main idea.)	No (But from the context of the paragraph, we might guess that powers means *multiples*; multiplication formulas showing "20" follow this word.)	Noun
4. decimal	No (The word appears only once, and the information can be understood without understanding this word.)	Yes (line 11) Example. calculation with a base of 10	Noun
5. cocoa beans	No (The word appears only once, near the end, and is not directly related to the main idea of the reading.)	No (But the context tells us that it is something that merchants sold and that they used for counting.)	Noun

CHAPTER 8 85

Choices of additional unfamiliar words will vary. Possible unfamiliar, important word: *system*.

C. Predicting Ideas with Signal Words

1. a. contrast = instead of (lines 3, 15)
      = but (line 15)
   b. reason or cause = because (lines 8, 13)
   c. example = for example (line 11)
      here's an example (line 25)
2. Answers may vary, depending on the signal words that students identified.

D. Identifying the Main Idea

The main idea of the reading, which should be underlined, is in line 1: *The Maya had an excellent number system*. The comparison that helps make this idea clear is the comparison to the Arabic number system, which has some similarities.

Remember
Student Book p. 142

Picture notes may vary. They should follow the example in the reading and use bars and dots. Each number should be shown vertically.

Discuss
Student Book p. 142

Answers will vary.

CHAPTER 9
Reading Skills and Strategies

PART 1: COMPREHENSION STRATEGIES

Prepare

Predicting from First and Last Paragraphs
Student Book p. 144

ACTIVITY 1

Answers may vary. Possible predictions:

1. Topic: a summer trip walking the Appalachian Trail
   Main idea: how the experience of walking the Appalachian Trail changed their lives
2. Topic: parents, children, and exercise
   Main idea: parents must understand how much exercise their children are getting (or: parents must encourage their children to exercise more, because children don't get enough exercise)

Read

Understanding Supporting Details
Student Book p. 146

ACTIVITY 2

Main idea: The difficulty of having a successful job interview with Admiral Rickover.

Supporting details: Only one out of 100 men ever got hired. He had a special chair for the men he interviewed. Its front legs were shorter than its back legs. While the interviewee tried to stay in the chair, the admiral asked him many difficult questions.

Types of details: statistic, example

ACTIVITY 3

1. (b) and (c) should be circled.
   The detail in (a) proves the opposite point. The detail in (d) offers no support for the main idea.
2. (a) and (c) should be circled.
   The detail in (b) is not related to the point. The detail in (d) offers no support for the main idea.
3. (b) should be circled.
   The detail in (a) offers no support (it's entirely subject to personal opinion, and therefore hard to prove as a point). The detail in (c) offers no support for the main idea. The detail in (d) offers no support (why should the high salary of players justify making it the national sport?).

Using Connectors to Follow Ideas
Student Book p. 149

ACTIVITY 4

The missing words appear in boldface below:

1. My brother is fun-loving, but **he is also** responsible.
2. Meryl is going to be a doctor, or **she is going to be** a nurse.
3. I gave you that money to pay your rent and **to pay** your bills.

ACTIVITY 5

The ellipses should connect to the following words or phrases:

1. the baby horse's legs were; strong
2. he carried
3. good for you
4. but he's (not) going
5. American cowboys; American cowboys
6. the dishes

Using Signal Words to Predict Ideas
Student Book p. 150

ACTIVITY 6

1. Signal words: in spite of
   a. illness
2. Signal word: While
   c. can't leave home now
3. Signal word: by
   a. this evening
4. Signal words: In fact
   a. she never married anyone

ACTIVITY 7

Answers will vary. Possible predictions:

1. The president made his speech despite *his illness/despite the fact that nobody wanted to listen to it.*
2. Rain rarely falls in the Atacama Desert. In fact, *there were only two inches of rainfall last year./ In fact, it's so dry there that few animals can survive.*
3. Please don't open the door during *the concert/during the class presentations.*
4. While she never goes to the doctor, *she goes to the dentist twice a year./she always worries that she is sick.*
5. *The kids can't watch TV/My friends won't talk on the phone* until they have done their homework.

Making Inferences
Student Book p. 151

ACTIVITY 8

Answers will vary. Possible inferences: Sylvia didn't get a good grade on the test. Sylvia was worried about her grade. Mrs. Marple wasn't happy about Sylvia's grade. Sylvia wasn't happy about her grade.

ACTIVITY 9

1. a. No, a puppy is not always a good Christmas present.
   Facts: Puppies are a lot of work, they can cause damage in homes, and they need to go outside at inconvenient times.
   b. Only someone who understands all the responsibilities and risks of owning a puppy should get one.
   Facts: People who don't understand this get upset and get angry.

2. a. The speaker is a substitute teacher.

   Facts: The speaker refers to students, a regular teacher who is absent, and assignments.

   b. This person didn't like the job.

   Facts: The money wasn't bad, but the work was terrible. The students laughed. No one listened. They refused to do their assignments. They talked.

3. a. Caroline is a brave person who admires firefighters. She is ambitious.

   Facts: She decided to be a firefighter when she was ten years old. Her brother almost died in a fire that year. A young firefighter saved him.

   b. People laughed at her because she was a girl and she was young.

   Facts: She is referred to as a female; she was ten years old at the time. Also, the townspeople in this new town might not have known about the incident with her brother and the fire, which occurred in a different town.

Reading Difficult Material
Student Book p. 153

ACTIVITY 10

Students should be encouraged to use the reading strategies and to read the passage more than once.

Remember

Outlining
Student Book p. 154

ACTIVITY 11

Outlines may vary. Possible outline of Reading 2 in Chapter 3: "Shark Sense."

Main idea: Sharks are excellent hunters

I. Amazing sensory equipment
   A. Feeling
      1. can sense weak electricity from small fish breathing
      2. can notice even small change in environment
   B. Seeing
      1. has sensitive eyes, can see when there's little light
      2. moves head from side to side to see objects in front
   C. Smelling
      1. great sense of smell
      2. can smell very small amounts of blood in the water
   D. Hearing
      1. very sensitive ears
      2. can hear sounds 200 yards (500 meters) away; some hear farther

II. Very powerful
   A. Jaws
      1. are made of cartilage, not bone
      2. have several rows of teeth
      3. can bite with a pressure of 2,000 pounds per square inch (great white)
   B. Teeth
      1. has very sharp teeth
      2. replaces teeth when they are lost (teeth move forward)

CHAPTER 9

Using Grouping and Classification
Student Book p. 156

ACTIVITY 12

1. *The Empire State Building* and *the White House* are examples. > *Edifices* are a class of things. > The examples are both of buildings. > Therefore, *edifices* = buildings.

2. *No money* and *no education* are examples. > He succeeded despite the *constraints*—the constraints didn't stop him. > Therefore, *constraints* = things that can stop you or limit you; restrictions.

3. *sapphires* = one of four items listed > The list describes *beautiful gems*. > Gems are a class of things that are found in a necklace (jewelry). > Therefore, *sapphire* = a type of gem or jewel.

4. *cleome* = one of three items listed. > All are things that grow in a garden. > Plants (flowers) grow in a garden > Therefore, *cleome* = a type of plant or flower.

5. *such as* = signal word for examples. > *Steel, rice, oil,* and *wheat* = examples > They belong to the same class or group (*commodities*) of things, or products, that can be imported (bought from another country). > Therefore, *commodities* = group of things: products, things that can be bought and sold.

6. *parallelograms* and *trapezoids* = two of five items listed. > List describes things that someone learned about. > Other items in the list are more recognizable; they are shapes. > All items listed belong to the same class, or group. > *parallelograms* and *trapezoids* = examples of shapes.

Using a Dictionary
Student Book p. 157

ACTIVITY 13

1. beetle bill carport lump mask meaning soil unmask world

2. ear early eat egg enclose enemy equator extend extra

3. glacier glad glance glass glaze glib glide gloom gloss

ACTIVITY 14

1. like, limit, light
2. flavor, flex, fleece
3. catch, cat

ACTIVITY 15

1. b. Dancing when you get good news.
2. b. look for
3. c. are unhappy about it
4. b. happening before
5. a. only lasts a short while
6. a. makes people laugh
7. b. think fast

ACTIVITY 16

Answers may vary slightly, depending on the dictionary used.

1. began/initiated/started
2. a wreck/in bad shape/a mess
3. walked around in an angry way
4. unpredictable/unusual
5. news story/a lead on a news story/an inside tip about a news story to report on

Recognizing Abbreviations
Student Book p. 161

ACTIVITY 17

1. Doctor William Stanley, Doctor of Dentistry
2. Sunday, January 12, at 3:00 in the afternoon
3. 120 Apple Road, Post Office Box 320
4. Sergeant Julie McKenzie
5. Apartment B

ACTIVITY 18

The abbreviations that do NOT belong in each group are listed below:

1. Ms. (it is a title), Mon. (it is a day)
2. Mr. (it is a general title), P.M. (it is a time), Tu. (it is a day), Rd. (it is an address)
3. Wed. (it is a day), Thur. (it is a day), Mar. (it is a month), Apr. (it is a month)
4. P.O. (it is an address), Mr. (it is a title), Ave. (it is an address), Sgt. (it is a title/profession)
5. Bldg. (it is an address), M.D. (it is a profession), Sat. (it is a day)
6. hr. (it is a time), blvd. (it is an address); answers will vary for "hr." since it is a measurement of time

ACTIVITY 19

The items that are NOT abbreviations are: Go., Sit.

Reading: Along the Silk Road

Getting Started
Student Book p. 164

1. Answers will vary. Possible answers: The Silk Road is in Asia. (China). It is famous because many people used it at one time to travel between East and West.
2. Answers may vary. Possible answers: It may be called the Silk Road because people transported or traded silk along this road. The road may have connected to a country or region where silk was made.

Prepare
Student Book p. 165

Answers may vary. Possible answers:

1. c. the misnaming of the Silk Road
2. The main idea is that the Silk Road is a romantic name but an incorrect one. The main idea can be found in the title as well as in the first and last paragraphs.
3. There will probably not be terms about love in the text. Although "romantic" is a word that relates to love and romance, the word here is used to describe a place, not a relationship between people. Also, the article will probably talk about why the name is not romantic.
4. Pre-reading questions will vary. Possible questions:
   - How did the Silk Road get its name?
   - What is the Silk Road?
   - Where is the Silk Road?
   - What was the Silk Road used for?

Read
Student Book p. 165

Answers to the possible prediction questions from the *Prepare* section:

- The Silk Road got its name from a 19th-century German historian, Ferdinand von Richthofen, who was the first to use that name.
- The Silk Road was a trade route.
- The Silk Road was between China and Europe.
- The Silk Road was used to carry silk and other commodities for trade.

Read Again
Student Book p. 166

Practice of individual reading strategies should be encouraged; answers will vary.

The main ideas and supporting details should be identified as follows:

Paragraph 1: The name "Silk Road" is used by nearly everyone.

Supporting details: Paragraph 1 explains what the name "Silk Road" makes people think of and the images it brings to mind.

Paragraph 2: However, the historian's term for this ancient route between China and Europe is not exactly correct.

Supporting details: The next few paragraphs explain that there was more than one route and that other commodities were also carried along the route.

Paragraph 3: First, there is more than one route.

Supporting details: Paragraph 3 explains that there were several branches of the route.

Paragraph 4: Two of the branch routes were especially popular.

Supporting details: Paragraph 4 explains the northern and southern routes.

Paragraph 5: Second, silk was not all that the caravans carried, although silk was the most remarkable commodity for the people of the West.

Supporting details: Paragraph 5 says that silk was the most remarkable commodity, as the Romans didn't see silk until they were fighting the Parthians.

Paragraph 6: The name "Silk Road" is a misnomer especially because, in addition to silk, the route carried many other costly commodities.

Supporting details: Paragraph 6 lists the other goods: gold, precious stones, ceramics, jade, bronze objects, iron, etc.

Paragraph 7: Although the term "Silk Road" continues to be popular today, it is nonetheless misleading.

Supporting details: This paragraph sums up the article, so the supporting details have already been given in Paragraphs 3–6.

For connectors and signal words, see *C. Following Ideas* and *D. Predicting Ideas with Signal Words* on TM page 92.

Yes, the conclusion sums up the reading.

Post-Reading Activities

A. Comprehension Check

1. Students can make and label a simple line drawing in their notebooks or label their books. See the map on Student Book p. 166 for location of the places.
2. The Silk Road got its name from a 19th-century German historian, Ferdinand von Richthofen, who was the first to use that name.
3. The name "Silk Road" is romantic because it brings to mind images of ancient caravans along a desert road, every camel carrying large bundles of the soft, beautiful cloth.
4. The most popular Silk Road routes were the northern and the southern.
5. In addition to silk, the caravans carried many other costly commodities: gold and other precious metals, ivory, precious stones, glass, furs, ceramics, jade, bronze objects, lacquer, and iron.

B. Vocabulary Check

1. Some words may have more than one type of context clue:
   a. grammar: commodities, furs, goods (all plural nouns)
   b. grouping: ivory, furs, lacquer (all items in a group or class); commodities (the name of the group or class)
   c. internal definition: commodities, goods (synonyms)

2. The chart should be completed as follows:

Word	Prefix	Suffix	Part of speech	Meaning
a. misnamed	mis-	-ed	adjective	having the wrong or incorrect name
b. misnomer	mis-	-er	noun	the wrong name
c. misleading	mis-	-ing	adjective	giving people the wrong idea

3. Two synonyms for *expensive* in the reading are *costly* and *precious* (line 34).

4. Answers for some categories, such as "Can I use world knowledge?" will vary. Some sections of the chart may be completed as follows:

Word	Is it important?	Is there an internal definition?	It is a noun? verb? adjective?
1. caravan	Yes (The word repeats, and it appears in the introduction and the topic sentences.)	Yes (line 2) *every camel carrying large bundles*	Noun
2. bundle	No (The word is used only once, and it is not directly related to the main idea of the paragraph or the reading.)	No	Noun
3. trade	Yes (The word repeats, both as a noun and a verb, and is directly related to the main idea.)	No (But from context, we can guess that it is an activity involving buying and selling commodities.)	Noun and verb
4. trader	Yes (The word repeats, both in this form and in another word form, and is directly related to the main idea.)	No (But from context, we can guess that it means a person who trades—who buys or sells commodities. See lines 36–37: *Traders bought goods in one place, traveled over part of the route, and sold them to another trader.*)	Noun (person)

Word	Is it important?	Is there an internal definition?	It is a noun? verb? adjective?
5. remarkable	No (The word appears in a topic sentence, but it is used only once—in a contrasting clause—and is not directly related to the main idea. Also it's a description word.)	No	Adjective
6. route	Yes (The word repeats and is used in topic sentences.)	Yes (line 8) Synonym: *road*	Noun

Choices of additional unfamiliar words will vary. Possible unfamiliar, important words: *ancient, desert, mental, historian, divided, branches, branched off, merchants, network.*

5. **a.** foot: bottom of the Pamir Mountains (a foot is literally a part of the body, but here it refers to the bottom of the mountains)
   b. corridor: the Gansu Corridor (a corridor is a hallway in a building, but here it refers to a passage through mountains)
   c. branch: the northern and southern routes (a branch is literally part of a tree, but here it is a division of a road, where a smaller road separates and departs from a main road)

C. Following Ideas

The omitted words that fill in the ellipsis appear in boldface:

1. China's trade routes to the West generally started at one of two places, **they started at** Loyang or **they started at** Changan.
2. The southern route branched off at Dunhuang, **the route** passed through the Yang Guan, and **the route** followed the southern edge of the desert, through Miran, Hetian, and Shache.

D. Predicting Ideas with Signal Words

1. **a.** addition = in addition to (line 33)
      = also (line 35)
   b. balancing contrasting points = while (line 40)
   c. emphasizing similar points = In fact (lines 5–6)
   d. time or sequence = First (line 7)
      = Second (line 29)

2. Answers may vary. Possible restatements of the ideas the signal words connect:
   a. The name "Silk Road" is a misnomer especially because, **besides (OR along with)** silk, the route carried many other costly commodities. Caravans to China carried gold and other precious metals, ivory, precious stones, and glass. From China, traders carried furs, ceramics, jade, bronze objects, lacquer, and iron **as well.**
   b. **Although** silk was an important commodity, it was certainly not the only one that traders carried.
   c. The historian's term for this ancient route between China and Europe is not exactly correct. It's **actually** misleading. **(OR Indeed/As a matter of fact,** it's misleading).
   d. **Number one**, there is more than one route. **(OR The first reason** is that there is more than one route.) **Number two**, silk was not all the caravans carried. **(OR The second reason** is that silk was not all the caravans carried.)

E. Identifying Main Ideas and Supporting Details

1. The main idea of this reading is that "Silk Road" is an incorrect and misleading name for the ancient trade route between China and Europe.
2. The two main supporting details are that there is not just one route—there is more than one—and the route carried many commodities besides silk.

Remember
Student Book p. 170

Outlines may vary. Possible outline: The Silk Road

I. Definition
   an ancient trade route between China and Europe
II. How it got its name
   A. A 19th-century German historian used this name
   B. The name is still popular today
III. Why the name is misleading
   A. There is more than one road—there is a network of roads
   B. Silk was not the only commodity that was carried and traded along this route

Discuss
Student Book p. 170

1. Answers will vary. Possible answers: Historically, other trade routes were between Britain, America, and the West Indies. There were trade routes through India and Africa, and between Europe and America. Today there is free trade across North American borders (among Mexico, the United States, and Canada).
2. Answers may vary. Possible answer: Yes, trade was important in the ancient world because there was not a system of money like we have today. People had to exchange goods. It was also much more difficult to travel in the ancient world—it took a lot longer—and so goods had to be sold and transported to places that could not grow or manufacture them. People could not easily go to those places and get these goods themselves; traders had to bring them in and merchants had to sell them.

Prepare
Student Book p. 170

Answers may vary. Possible answers:

1. Marco Polo was an explorer. He was the son of a businessman from Venice, Italy, in the 1200s.
2. Possible terms related to Polo's adventures in China: *explore, trade, discover, navigate, journey, stories, tales.*
3. The reading will probably say that Marco Polo did not go to China. The subtitle suggests that his adventures may be *fiction*, meaning they may not be true.

Read
Student Book p. 171

Possible answer to the prediction question from the *Prepare* section:

- There is some evidence to suggest that he did not actually go to China, but it is not certain if he did or did not go.

Read Again
Student Book p. 172

Practice of individual reading strategies should be encouraged; answers will vary.

The reading's main idea is stated in line 40: Today, not everyone believes that Marco Polo visited China.
Possible restatement of the idea: It is possible that Marco Polo didn't actually go to China.

For connectors and signal words, see *C. Following Ideas* on TM page 95 and *D. Predicting Ideas with Signal Words* on TM page 96.

The conclusion does not entirely sum up the reading. It states the main idea related to the title, but it does not sum up all the facts of Marco Polo's journeys (or those of his family) mentioned earlier in the reading.

Post-Reading Activities

A. Comprehension Check

1. **a.** 1260 **b.** 1269 **c.** 1271 **d.** 1274 **e.** 1291
2. People didn't believe Marco Polo because they thought he made up information with stories from other people. He didn't mention important aspects of Chinese culture. Kublai Khan's records don't mention him or his family.
3. Marco Polo met Rustichello in prison.
4. Rustichello was a writer of romance stories.

B. Vocabulary Check

1. Related word forms and parts of speech:
   a. civilize (v) = civilization (line 35; noun)
      = civilized (line 36; adjective)
   b. communicate (v) = communication (line 5; noun)
   c. Venice (n) = Venetians (line 24; noun = people from Venice)
      = Venetian (line 25; adjective)
2. Three examples of foreign peoples the Polos met: *Persians, Turks,* and *Mongols.* The phrase that groups these peoples: *people from many other cultures.*
3. Answers for some categories, such as "Can I use world knowledge?" will vary. Some sections of the chart may be completed as follows:

Word	Is it important?	Is there an internal definition?	It is a noun? verb? adjective?
1. journey	Yes (The word repeats.)	Yes (lines 3, and elsewhere) Synonym: *trip*	Noun
2. arrival	Yes (The word appears in a topic sentence.)	Yes (line 27) Related word: *reached*	Noun
3. prison	Yes (The word relates to the main idea of the paragraph.)	No (But we can guess from the context; he was captured by an enemy and sent there.)	Noun
4. falconer	No (The word does not repeat and it is not directly related to the main idea of the paragraph or of the article.)	No	Noun
5. made up	Yes (It relates to the main idea, and a synonym is given.)	Yes (line 44) Synonym: *invented*	Verb

Word	Is it important?	Is there an internal definition?	It is a noun? verb? adjective?
6. Persia	No (It is a specific place name—a country—and not directly related to the main idea.)	No	Noun
7. disbelief	Yes (It is related to the main idea, and it is supported with examples in the paragraph.)	Yes (line 40) Contrasting idea: *not everyone believes*	Noun

Choices of additional unfamiliar words will vary. Possible unfamiliar, important words: *court, explorers, captured, printing presses, popularity, amazed, dog handlers, aspects, gunpowder.*

C. Following Ideas

1. The omitted words that fill in the ellipsis appear in boldface:
   According to Marco Polo, China was more civilized **than Europe, China was** far richer **than Europe**, and **China was** more advanced **than Europe**.

2. The reference chart should be completed as follows:

Word or Phrase	Line	Refers to
1. that time	4	1260
2. them	11	China and Europe
3. there	11	China
4. this time	18	a second journey to China (two years later)
5. it	21	X (subject of the sentence; no referent)
6. her	25	a Mongol princess
7. there	29	prison
8. it	35	the book
9. that	38	X (introduces a noun clause; no referent)

D. Predicting Ideas with Signal Words

1. so 2. In fact 3. Despite 4. First

E. Identifying Main Ideas and Supporting Details

1. Topic of paragraphs 1–4: the travels of Marco Polo and his family **(OR)** their adventures in China

   Topic of paragraphs 5-7: the debate over Marco Polo's book about his travels **(OR)** Are his adventures fact or fiction?

1271	1274	1295	1295	1295?	1295? +
Traveled to China with Father and Uncle	Arrived in China; lived and worked there for 17 years	Returned to Venice	Venice was at war with Genoa	Genoans sent Marco Polo to prison	He met Rustichello in prison and wrote a book.

the events of Marco Polo's life:

Discuss
Student Book p. 175

1. Answers may vary. Possible answers: Marco Polo did not travel to China. The article gives strong examples to support this. He wrote his book with the help of a romance writer, who wrote fiction. **(OR)** Yes, he did. He lived in China for so many years; he could not possibly have included every little detail about his experience or about Chinese culture. His quote—"I told less than half of what I actually know"—would support this. Maybe he himself did not know about all these details of Chinese culture. Also, there might be some other reason why Kublai Khan's records don't mention Marco Polo or his family.
2. Answers will vary.

Prepare
Student Book p. 175

Answers may vary. Possible answers:

2. The main idea of paragraph 7: Today, not everyone believes that Marco Polo visited China.
3. Supporting details: Marco Polo did not mention important aspects of Chinese culture such as the Great Wall of China, tea, or gunpowder. In addition, Kublai Khan's records do not mention Marco Polo or his father or uncle.

Remember
Student Book p. 175

Timelines may vary. Possible timeline illustrating

1. This reading is probably from an encyclopedia. The word "silk" is used as a title; there is no subtitle or author. There are headings dividing the text into sections. An illustration helps to show the process of making silk. The purpose of the reading seems to be to inform readers about silk, its history, and its production process.
2. The reading is probably not too difficult. The sections, headings, and illustrations help to make the information clear. Not all the sentences are long and complex (though some are), and some key words seem to be defined.
3. Possible terms related to silk and the process of making silk: *worms, larvae, cocoons, thread, raise, industry, factory.*
4. Pre-reading questions will vary. Possible questions:
   - When was silk first discovered?
   - What is silk made from?
   - What is silk used for?
   - Why is silk so valuable?

Read
Student Book p. 175

Answers to the possible prediction questions from

the *Prepare* section:

- According to legend, silk was first discovered in 2640 B.C.
- Silk is made from silkworms, which spin a cocoon; the silk threads can be removed from the cocoon.
- Silk can be used for various fabrics, as well as ribbon, lace, thread, and stockings.
- Silk is valuable because it is beautiful, light, and very strong.

Read Again
Student Book p. 176

Practice of individual reading strategies should be encouraged; answers will vary.

The main idea of each section should be identified as follows:

Section 1 (History): Legend says that Chinese Empress Hsi Ling-Shi discovered silk in 2640 B.C.

Section 2 (Production): Silk is made from the cocoon of the silkworm.

For connectors and signal words, see *C. Following Ideas* and *D. Predicting Ideas with Signal Words* on TM page 99.

Post-Reading Activities

A. Comprehension Check

The steps of the silk-making process should be placed in the following order:

1	Silkworms eat mulberry leaves.
2	Silkworms wrap themselves in the thread.
3	Silkworms make cocoons.
4	Workers put the cocoons in hot water.
5	Workers unwind the thread.
6	The threads are woven into cloth.

B. Vocabulary Check

Answers for some categories, such as "Can I use world knowledge?" will vary. Some sections of the chart may be completed as follows:

Word	Is it important?	Is there an internal definition?	It is a noun? verb? adjective?
1. legend	Yes (It is the first word of the reading.)	Yes (line 4) *this story may or may not be true*	Noun
2. accidentally	No (It is a description word for a verb, and it is only used once.)	No (But we can guess from the context that she didn't intend to this; *accidentally* means without plan or intention.)	Adverb
3. cocoon	Yes (The word repeats, appears in topic sentences, and relates to the main idea.)	Yes (line 18) Synonym: *larva*; (also paragraph 3) explanation for the process and materials of cocoons	Noun
4. unwound	Yes (The word relates to the main idea, describing part of the process.)	Yes (line 20) Antonym: *wound*; (lines 14–15) Definition: *wraps . . . by turning round and round*	Verb (here, it appears in the passive voice—the past participle of the *unwind* is used)

Word	Is it important?	Is there an internal definition?	It is a noun? verb? adjective?
5. thread	Yes (The word relates to the main idea, appears in topic sentences, and repeats.)	No (But we may guess from the context that it is produced by the silkworm—or it can be artificially made—and it is used for weaving into materials for fabrics.)	Noun
6. discovered	Yes (The word appears in the first sentence, and it repeats in different forms.)	No (But we may guess from the context that it means *found*.)	Verb
7. discovery	Yes (The word repeats in different forms.)	No (But we may guess from the context that it means a *finding*.)	Noun
8. sericulture	Yes (It is defined in the text and it relates to the main idea.)	Yes (lines 9–10) *the raising of silkworms*	Noun
9. loosens	Yes (The word is part of the process described, which relates to the main idea.)	No (Though we may guess from context that it means to make something loose, or not tight.)	Verb
10. weaving	Yes (The word relates to the end of the process described, the main idea.)	No	Noun (it looks like a verb in the *-ing* or progressive form—but it is in fact a gerund, and it's acting like a noun here as the object of a preposition)
11. fabric	Yes (The word relates to the end of the process described, the main idea.)	Yes (line 23) Examples: *chiffon, satin, velvet*	Noun
12. synthetic	No (The word does not repeat, appears only at the very end, and is not critical for understanding the main idea of the paragraph or of the reading.)	No (But we may guess from context that it means artificially made, not natural.)	Adjective

Choices of additional unfamiliar words will vary. Possible unfamiliar, important words: *remarkably, industry, glands, hardens, chiffon, satin, velvet.*

C. Following Ideas

The omitted words that fill in the ellipsis appear in boldface:

1. The silkworms stop eating, and **the silkworms** begin to make silk cocoons.
2. It takes about 1,000 cocoons for **them to make** one shirt and 3,000 **cocoons for them** to make one pound (454 g) of silk thread.

D. Predicting Ideas with Signal Words

1. While 2. during 3. also

E. Identifying Main Ideas and Supporting Details

The main idea of the reading is: Silk is made from the cocoon of the silkworm (line 8). It is not stated in the first and last paragraphs. This is because the reading is not an essay with a traditional introduction and conclusion. It is an encyclopedia entry (or an excerpt from one) divided into sections.

Remember
Student Book p. 178

Graphic organizers may vary. The most logical graphic organizer to show the silk-making process would be a flowchart:

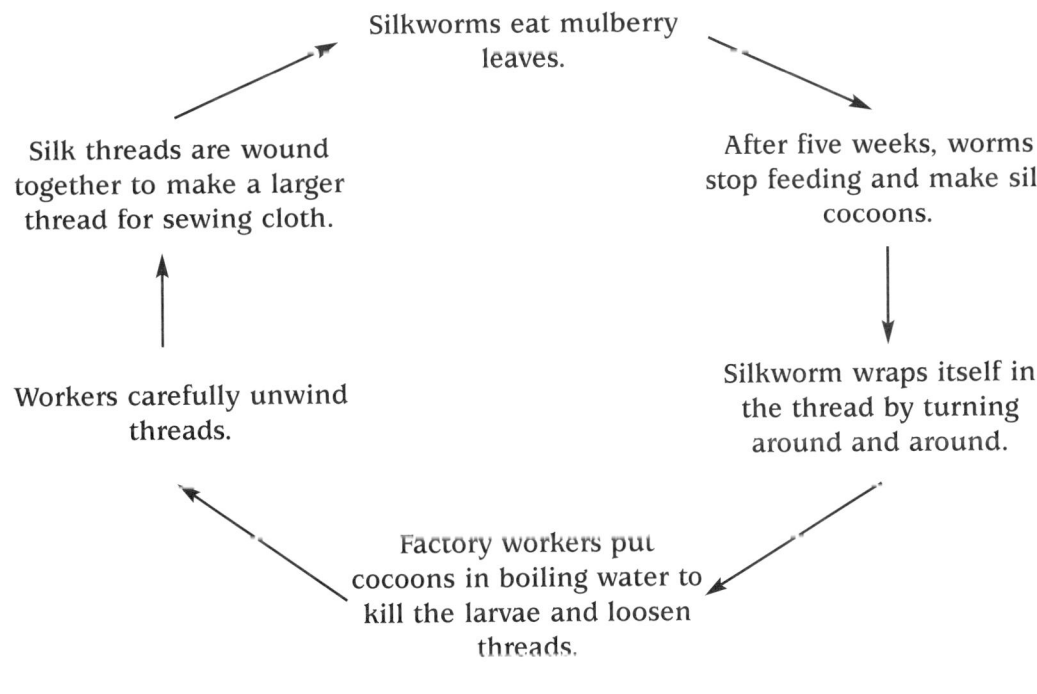

READING 4

Discuss
Student Book p. 178

1. Answers will vary.
2. Answers will vary. Possible answers: Clothes can be made of rayon, nylon, cotton, wool, leather, suede, and many other materials.

Prepare
Student Book p. 179

Answers may vary. Possible answers:

1. This is a brochure, specifically a travel brochure. There is information at the bottom about the price of a trip, the Website address and name of an adventure tours company, and other contact information. The title also sounds

like an advertisement for a trip or a tour.

2. This brochure is written for people who are interested in travel, and who may want to visit this region.

3. Answers will vary.

4. Pre-reading questions will vary. Possible questions:

   - How much does a tour of the Silk Road cost?
   - What are some of the places that the Silk Road tour visits?
   - What else can you do on this tour besides visiting the Silk Road?

- The Silk Road tour visits famous mountain ranges, beautiful towns, cities along the ancient Silk Road, and popular tourist attractions in China.

- You can hike, bike, ride on a camel, and visit the army of 6,000 life-size terracotta warriors that guard an emperor's tomb.

Read

Student Book p. 179

Answers to the possible prediction questions from the *Prepare* section:

- A tour of the Silk Road costs $3,500.00.

Read Again

Student Book p. 180

Practice of individual reading strategies should be encouraged; answers will vary.

For the most important attractions of each place, see *A. Comprehension Check* on TM page XX.

For connectors and signal words, see *C. Following Ideas* and *D. Predicting Ideas with Signal Words* on TM page XX.

Post-Reading Activities

A. Comprehension Check

The chart should be completed as follows:

Place	Country	Important Information
1. Rawalpindi	Pakistan	beginning of the tour
2. Himalayas	between Pakistan and China	peaks that reach 7,000–8,000 meters; including K2, the second highest mountain in the world
3. the Karakorum Highway	between Pakistan and China	built by the Chinese and the Pakistanis; is the backbone of two incredible mountain ranges
4. the Hunza Valley	between Pakistan and China	known for friendly people and beautiful scenery
5. Kashgar	China	an ancient Silk Road city
6. Urumqi	China	farther from the sea than any other city
7. Turpan	China	over 500 feet below sea level; one of the most important Silk Road stops

Place	Country	Important Information
8. Dunhuang	China	where the Silk Road divided
9. Xian	China	eastern end of the Silk Road, and the most popular tourist attraction in China (6,000 terracotta warriors)

B. Vocabulary Check

1. pass   2. pass through   3. spine   4. 4

5. Answers for some categories, such as "Can I use world knowledge?" will vary. Some sections of the chart may be completed as follows:

Word	Is it important?	Is there an internal definition?	It is a noun? verb? adjective?
1. incredible	Yes (A synonym/related word appears) OR: No (It is a description word.)	Yes (line 5) Synonym: *amazing*	Adjective
2. endless	No (It is a description word, does not repeat.)	No (But by analyzing the word form—the suffix *less*—we can guess the meaning: *without end*.)	Adjective
3. border	Yes (The word appears in a topic sentence, and makes it clear where the tour goes.)	No (But we can guess from context; the tour has been in Pakistan and now it is crossing over into China. A *border* is a line or separation between two countries.)	Noun
4. flight	No (The word does not repeat, does not appear in a topic sentence, and is not directly related to the main idea—it is not describing a place.)	No	Noun
5. divided	Yes (It appears in a sentence giving information about an important stop on the tour.)	No (But we can guess from context, and from the word *different*, line 28, that it has to do with separating.)	Verb

102 CHAPTER 10

Word	Is it important?	Is there an internal definition?	It is a noun? verb? adjective?
6. sand dunes	Yes (It appears in a sentence giving information about an important stop on the tour.) **OR:** No (The word does not repeat, and it does not appear in a topic sentence.)	No	Noun
7. terracotta	Yes (It appears in a sentence giving information about an important stop on the tour.) **OR:** No (The word does not repeat, and it does not appear in a topic sentence.)	No	Noun (here, either part of a compound noun, *terracotta warriors*, or considered an adjective, describing the warriors)
8. guard	Yes (It appears in a sentence giving information about an important stop on the tour.) **OR:** No (The word does not repeat, and it does not appear in a topic sentence.)	No	Verb
9. tomb	Yes (It appears in a sentence giving information about an important stop on the tour.) **OR:** No (The word does not repeat, and it does not appear in a topic sentence.)	No (But we can guess from the context that a tomb is a place where someone is buried; in lines 34–35 we learn that the tomb belongs to China's first Emperor, who clearly is no longer alive.)	Noun

Choices of additional unfamiliar words will vary.
Possible unfamiliar, important words: *ranges, climbs, edge, attraction.*

CHAPTER 10 **103**

C. Following Ideas

The reference chart should be completed as follows:

Word or Phrase	Line	Refers to
1. there	3	Rawalpindi
2. this amazing road	5	the famous Karakoram Highway
3. these mountains	7	the Himalayas and the Hindu Kush
4. this modern city	21	Urumqi
5. there	25	Turpan
6. we	28	X (subject of the sentence; no referent)

D. Predicting Ideas with Signal Words

1. a. after = line 17
   b. also = line 20
   c. finally = line 30
   d. then = line 13

2. a. after = connects the chronology of two events: *we cross the world's highest international border* as the first event and *we will travel through ancient Silk Road cities* as the second event.
   Possible restatement: We will cross the world's highest international border; **then** we will travel through ancient Silk Road cities . . .

   b. also = connects the additional city *Urumqi* to the list of cities in the previous statement: *Karakol, Tashkurgan, and Kashgar.*
   Possible restatement: . . . we will travel through ancient Silk Road cities . . . Additionally, we will stop in Urumqi . . .

   c. finally = connects the last place on the tour (*Xian—the eastern end of the Silk Road*) to all of the preceding places and ancient cities on the tour.
   Possible restatement: At last we arrive in Xian . . . (OR) Eventually we arrive in Xian.

   d. then = connects the chronology of events: *we will follow the River Indus to Gilgit* as the first event and *we will pass through the Hunza Valley* as the second event.
   Possible restatement: . . . we will follow the River Indus to Gilgit . . . After that, we will pass through the Hunza Valley

E. Making Inferences

Possible inference: "Real" mountains means mountains that are truly high or mountains that the tour is actually traveling through. The mountains that were referred to before this were impressive, but they were only viewed from a distance.

Remember
Student Book p. 183

Illustrations of the Silk Road tour route may vary. Illustrations should include two countries, China and Pakistan, separated by mountains (two mountains ranges); they should also include all the places listed in the chart in *A. Comprehension Check*. They may also include important information about each place.

104 CHAPTER 10

Discuss
Student Book p. 183

1. Answers will vary.

2. Answers will vary. Possible answer to the second part of the question: Travel writers get paid (usually) to go to different places and write about their experiences. They may write articles or guidebooks. They may write for Websites. Sometimes they take pictures too.

Reading: Hurray for Hollywood!

Getting Started
Student Book p. 185

Answers may vary. Possible answers:
1. Hollywood is a place where movies are made. It is in California, in the United States, near Los Angeles.
2. Hollywood is famous because so many movies are made there, and many famous actors and actresses live there.
3. Tourists go there to see the famous "Hollywood" sign (white letters on a hillside), to tour movie studios and sets, to see the street where famous actors have a gold star in the sidewalk.

Prepare
Student Book p. 186

Answers may vary. Possible answers:

1. The "sign of the stars" is a famous landmark or tourist attraction. It is the Hollywood sign. (This is suggested by the title, the first paragraph, and the last paragraph.)
2. The main idea is probably the history of the famous Hollywood sign. The genre of the reading is a magazine article. (It says "Travel Magazine" at the top of the page. Also, the sentences are not very long or complex; it seems to be written for a general audience.)
3. Possible terms related to the "Hollywood" sign: *famous, landmark, letters, hills, symbol, tourist attraction.*
4. The text will probably talk about the history of the famous Hollywood sign—how it got there, why it was placed there, what changes may have occurred. Possible questions:
   - Where is the sign?
   - Who put the sign there?
   - When was the sign put there?
   - How can you see the sign? (How can you get there?)

Read
Student Book p. 186

Answers to the possible prediction questions from the *Prepare* section:
- The sign is in the Hollywood Hills.
- The sign was originally put up by the Hollywoodland Real Estate Company.
- The sign was put up in 1923. It was repaired and rebuilt in 1978.
- You can see the sign from the city streets of Hollywood, or from your own home, on the Internet. You cannot travel to the sign or hike up to it; it is illegal.

Read Again
Student Book p. 187

Practice of individual reading strategies should be encouraged; answers will vary.

The main idea of each paragraph should be identified as follows:

Paragraph 1: One of the most famous landmarks in the world is now nearly impossible to see, but we can still learn about its famous history.

Paragraph 2: The sign we see today is not the same one that the Hollywoodland Real Estate Company put up in 1923.

Paragraph 3: The Hollywoodland sign became a symbol of the hopes and dreams of actors and actresses.

Paragraph 4: (The main idea is implied, not stated directly): When the Hollywoodland Real Estate Company went out of business, the sign was given to Los Angeles but it was not maintained.

Paragraph 5: By the early 1970s, it was clear that the sign needed more repairs.

Paragraph 6: (The main idea is implied, not stated directly): The sign was repaired in 1978.

Paragraph 7: Unfortunately, many who come to see it never do.

Paragraph 8: Now, however, there is one sure way to see the sign.

For connectors and signal words, see *C. Following Ideas* and *D. Predicting Ideas with Signal Words* on TM page 106.

Post-Reading Activities

A. Comprehension Check

1. T 2. F 3. F 4. F 5. F
6. T 7. F 8. F

B. Vocabulary Check

1. "stop doing business" = *went out of business* (line 27)
2. *ft.* (lines 9, 43) = feet; *lbs* (line 44) = pounds
3. *illegal* = not legal; prefix = *–il* (line 49)
4. *remove* (verb, line 32), *repairs* (noun, line 35), *rebuild* (verb, line 36)

   Note: Students may incorrectly identify *real* (from *Real Estate*) as one of the words with a *re–* prefix. In this word, *re–* is not a prefix.
5. *Demolished* is pronounced \di–ma′–lisht\.
6. Answers for some categories, such as "Can I use world knowledge?" will vary. Some sections of the chart may be completed as follows:

Word	Is it important?	Is there an internal definition?	It is a noun? verb? adjective?
1. landmark	Yes (It is part of the title and it appears in the first paragraph.)	No (But we can guess from the context that it is a tourist attraction, or something important to see in a place.)	Noun
2. erected	Yes (It relates to the main idea of the paragraph, and a synonym is given.)	Yes (line 6) Synonym: *put up*	Verb
3. Chamber of Commerce	Yes (Although it is a specific name of something, it repeats and it relates to the main idea.)	No (But we can guess from the context that it has something to do with business, or the organization of businesses.)	Noun
4. repairs	Yes (Synonyms/ related words are used, and it relates to the main idea.)	Yes (line 31) Synonym: *fix*	Noun

106 CHAPTER 11

Word	Is it important?	Is there an internal definition?	It is a noun? verb? adjective?
5. rebuild	Yes (Synonyms/related words are used, and it relates to the main idea.)	No (But we can guess from the context that it is related to *repairs* and *fix*; also, the prefix *re-* means *again*; here, the word means *build again*.)	Verb
6. donors	No (The word does not repeat, and the main idea of the paragraph is clear without understanding this word.)	No (But there is an example of a donor, Alice Cooper, who bought a letter to support the rebuilding of the Hollywood sign; also, the word "*sold*", line 37, appears in quotations, suggesting that it has a special meaning here.)	Noun
7. disappointed	Yes (It's a description word, but it relates to the main idea of the paragraph.)	Yes (line 19) Related words: *sadly*; (also lines 24–25): *broken dreams*	Adjective

Choices of additional unfamiliar words will vary. Possible unfamiliar, important words: *real estate, symbol, ladder, broken, troubles, demolished, steel, attracts, in person, arrested, fine, traffic jams.*

7. Class of tourist: people who want to see the sign in person

Examples: some try to hike it; some try to drive into town

C. Following Ideas

The reference chart should be completed as follows:

Words	Line	Refers to
1. there	21	the Hollywood sign
2. that point	30	the H fell over one day in 1949
3. this	33	the H fell over one day in 1949

D. Predicting Ideas with Signal Words

1. a. emphasizing similar points = In fact (line 13)

   b. making a point clear = In other words (line 52)

   c. time and sequence = At that time (line 7)
   = In 1932 (lines 17–18)
   = In 1944 (line 26)
   = in 1949 (lines 29–30)
   = At that point (line 30)
   = By the early 1970s (lines 33–34)
   = in August 1978 (line 40)
   = in November (line 41)
   = Every year (line 45)
   = Now (line 54)

2. Answers may vary, depending on the signal words that students identified in #1.

E. Identifying Main Ideas and Supporting Details

The chart should be completed as follows:

Paragraph	Main Idea	Supporting Details
1	One of the most famous landmarks in the world is now nearly impossible to see, but we can still learn about its famous history.	No supporting details
2	The sign we see today is not the same one that the Hollywoodland Real Estate Company put up in 1923.	**Fact:** The original sign was put up in 1923 by the Hollywoodland Real Estate Company. **Fact:** It advertised land in Hollywood Hills.
3	The Hollywoodland sign became a symbol of the hopes and dreams of actors and actresses. However, the history of the Hollywoodland sign shows that dreams do not always come true.	**Example:** In 1932, a young actress named Peg Entwhistle was sadly disappointed because she was not successful. Ms. Entwhistle hiked to the Hollywoodland sign. There, she found a ladder by the letter H. She climbed to the top and jumped to her death.
4	(The main idea is implied, not stated directly): The sign was neglected between 1944 and 1949.	**Fact:** In 1944, the Hollywoodland Real Estate Company went out of business. **Fact:** The owners gave the sign to the city of Los Angeles. **Fact:** No one was interested in it until the H fell over one day in 1949. **Fact:** At that point, the Hollywood Chamber of Commerce offered to fix the sign. They also decided to remove the last four letters.
5	By the early 1970s, it was clear that the sign needed more repairs.	**Fact:** The Chamber of Commerce started raising money to rebuild it. **Fact:** Chamber of Commerce businesses "sold" letters to donors for $27,700 each. **Example:** Rock star Alice Cooper bought an "O."

Paragraph	Main Idea	Supporting Details
6	(The main idea is implied, not stated directly): The sign was repaired in 1978.	**Fact:** Work on the sign began in August 1978 and was finished in November. **Fact:** The old sign was demolished, and new steel letters were put in its place. **Description:** The sign is now 450 ft. wide but still 50 ft. tall. It weighs 450,000 pounds.
7	Unfortunately, many who come to see it never do.	**Example:** Some try to hike up to the sign but get arrested. This is illegal, and the police fine them. **Example:** Others try to drive into town. The view is good from the city streets but the traffic jams are terrible.
8	Now, however, there is one sure way to see the sign.	**Fact:** You can visit the official Website on the Internet. There, the world's most famous sign is now available for viewing 24 hours a day.

Remember
Student Book p. 190

Timelines may vary. Possible timeline:

1923	1932	1944	1949	early 1970s	August 1978	November 1978
The Hollywoodland Real Estate Co. put up a sign.	A young actress, Peg Entwhistle, jumped to her death from the sign.	The Hollywoodland Real Estate Co. went out of business; the owners gave the sign to Los Angeles.	The H fell over, and the Hollywood Chamber of Commerce offered to fix the sign.	The Chamber of Commerce raised money to rebuild the sign.	Work began on rebuilding the sign.	The rebuilding was done; the old sign was demolished.

Discuss
Student Book p. 190

1. Answers will vary. Possible answer: Disneyland (or Disneyworld) is sometimes considered a "land of dreams." It is advertised as a place of fantasy, a place where dreams come true. New York has often been considered a land of dreams. Many immigrants went to America in search of a new and better life, and many arrived (and stayed) in New York.

2. Answers to the possible additional prediction questions. Answers will vary.

Prepare
Student Book p. 190

Answers may vary. Possible answers:
1. The topic of the reading is movie credits/common terms related to movie credits.
2. Information is arranged as a list of terms. This is because a glossary defines key words; it is like a dictionary of terms related to a topic.
3. Possible jobs listed on movies: producer, director, editor, music director, art director, actor, actress, assistants, extras.
4. Possible additional questions:
   - Who tells the actors what to do?
   - What is another name for art director?

Read
Student Book p. 190

Possible answer to the prediction question from the *Prepare* section:
- A producer finds ideas for movies, hires the director, and works with the director to hire the actors. The producer also takes care of the money.

Answers to the possible additional prediction question:
- The director is the person who tells the actors what to do.
- The art director is also called the production designer.

Read Again
Student Book p. 191

Practice of individual reading strategies should be encouraged; answers will vary.

Possible additional questions and answers:
  Question: What does a director do?
  Answer: A director is in charge of making the film. He or she has complete artistic control over the movie, so plans the camera shots and tells the actors what to do.

  Question: How are the producer and director different?
  Answer: They work closely together. They hire the actors together. Usually, the producer handles the money and the director handles the artistic control of the film.

Post-Reading Activities

A. Comprehension Check

The diagram should be completed with the following job responsibilities. Information that should be supplied appears in boldface:

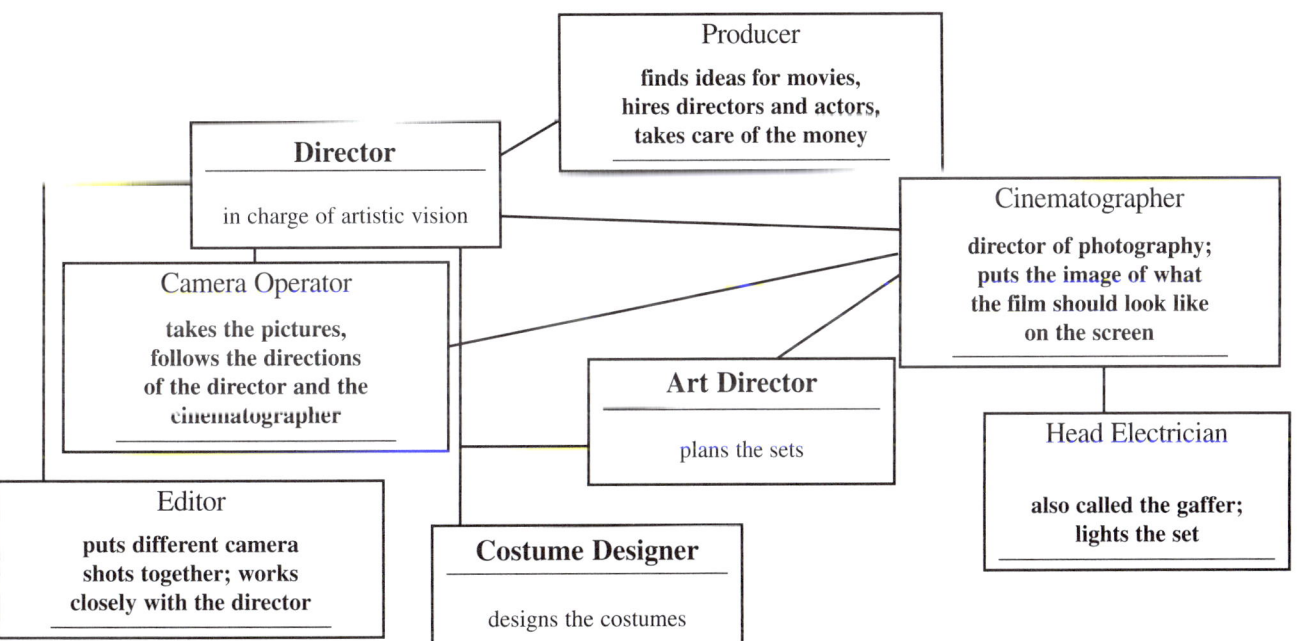

B. Vocabulary Check

1. a. *art* (n) = artistic (adj)
   b. *producer* (n) = production (n)
   c. *real* (adj) = realistic (adj)

2. The job names all have an *–or* or *–er* suffix. This is because these suffixes, when used for a noun, indicate a *person* who does that job or activity.

3. Answers for some categories, such as "Can I use world knowledge?" will vary. Some sections of the chart may be completed as follows:

Word	Is it important?	Is there an internal definition?	It is a noun? verb? adjective?
1. credits	Yes (The word appears in the title and the introduction paragraph.)	Yes (lines 1–2) *This is a list of the most important people who worked on the movie and their job description.*	Noun
2. in charge of	Yes (The word appears in a topic sentence about a job description.)	No (But we can guess from the context that it means *responsible for* or *in control of*.)	Adjective phrase
3. mental	No (It's a description word and it does not repeat.) OR: Yes (It is part of a job description and relates to the main idea of the description.)	No (But we might guess from context that it means a picture in one's mind, something that no one else can see.)	Adjective
4. image	Yes (The word repeats.)	No (But we might guess from context that it means *picture*, since the paragraph is about photography and visuals.)	Noun
5. sets	Yes (It relates to the main idea of the paragraph, it is a key part of the job description.)	No (But we might guess from context that *sets* have to do with where the scenes are filmed, the locations; knowing about *architecture* and *interior design* is important.)	Noun
6. create	Yes (It relates to the main idea of the paragraph; it is part of the job description.)	Yes (line 19) Synonym: *make*; (line 18) Antonym: *buy*	Verb

Word	Is it important?	Is there an internal definition?	It is a noun? verb? adjective?
7. research	No (It does not repeat.) OR: Yes (It is part of a job description and relates to the main idea of the description.)	No (But we might guess from context that research involves studying a particular time in the past, finding historical information related to the movie.)	Noun (can also be a verb)

Choices of additional unfamiliar words will vary. Possible unfamiliar, important words: *glossary, hire, shots, design, architecture, interior, particular, operator*.

C. Making Inferences

1. T (Since the director has complete artistic control over the movie, the art director needs to understand the director's ideas.)
2. X (The cinematographer MAY know something about electricity, since this position involves working with the gaffer—the head electrician. However, the cinematographer is more concerned with the science and art of photography, which does not necessarily require an understanding of electricity.)
3. F (The producer does not work directly with the gaffer or the cinematographer, people who are likely to know about lighting. The producer does not need an understanding of lighting in order to do his or her job.)

Remember

Student Book p. 192

Outlines may vary. Possible outline:

Glossary of Movie Credits

I. Producer
   A. Finds ideas for movies
   B. Hires the Director
      1. Works with the Director to hire actors
   C. Takes care of the money
II. Director
   A. Is in charge of making the film; has complete artistic control
      1. Plans the camera shots
      2. Has a mental image of what the film should look like
      3. Tells the actors what to do
   B. Works with the Producer to hire actors
III. Cinematographer
    Director of photography
   A. Knows about the art and science of photography
   B. Tries to put the director's mental image of the film on the screen
IV. Art Director
   A. Also called the Production Designer
   B. Designs sets
      1. Needs to know about architecture and interior design
   C. Works with the Cinematographer
V. Costume Designer
   A. Plans the clothes that the actors wear
      1. May create the clothes or buy them
      2. Often does research to make realistic clothing for a particular time
   B. Works with the Director and the Art Director
VI. Editor
   A. Puts different scene shots together
   B. Works closely with the Director
VII. Camera Operator
   A. Takes the pictures
   B. Follows the directions of the Director and the Cinematographer
VIII. Gaffer
   A. Also called the Head Electrician
   B. Responsible for lighting the set
   C. Works closely with the Cinematographer

112 CHAPTER 11

Discuss
Student Book p. 193

Answers will vary.

Prepare
Student Book p. 193

Answers may vary. Possible answers:
1. The features that suggest this reading is an interview: The names of two speakers alternate throughout the reading (it is a dialogue) and the first paragraph tells us that someone took time to talk with the author.
2. Mary Zophres is a costumer designer in Hollywood. (This information can be determined by skimming the first paragraph and the first line of the interview.)
3. You might become a costume designer by studying theater, costume design, or fashion; you may need a college degree. You might work part-time for a theater, film, or TV company to learn more about costume design or to meet people in the industry. Possible terms related to costume design: *material, fabric, history/historical, period, clothing, sew, theater, movies, film*.

Read
Student Book p. 193

Students should be encouraged to circle terms they listed in #3 of the *Prepare* section.

Read Again
Student Book p. 194

Practice of individual reading strategies should be encouraged; answers will vary.

Students should note that Janice, the interviewer, asks the questions, and Mary gives the main answer in the first line of each response. Mary then expands on her answers with supporting details and examples.

For connectors and their referents, see *C. Following Ideas* on TM page 114.

Signal words and predictions:
- *And* (lines 1, 3, 7, 8, 10, 13, 15, 18, 29, 32) indicates additional information.
- *Such as* (line 2) indicates an example.
- *The first time* (line 10) indicates time, chronology of events.
- *Then* (lines 13, 15) indicates time or chronology of events.
- *After* (line 14) indicates time or chronology of events.
- *First* (line 19) indicates time or chronology of events.
- *But* (lines 21, 23, 25, 31) indicates contrasting information.
- *For example* (line 28) indicates an example.
- *150 years ago* (line 32) indicates time or chronology of events.

Post-Reading Activities

A. Comprehension Check
1. T   2. F   3. T   4. T   5. F   6. F
7. T   8. F   9. F   10. T

B. Vocabulary Check
1. "to begin something" = *I was on my way* (line 21)
2. a. lifelong > life + long = throughout one's entire life
   b. moviemaking > movie + making = the process of making movies
   c. spotlight > spot + light = a light that illuminates or highlights one particular area or person
   d. yearbooks > year + books = books that come out each year at a school (usually high school and college), showing the pictures of people in each class and showing scenes of daily life at that time
3. The first syllable, *cor*, is stressed in *corset*. A dictionary will likely give this information. Also, many nouns stress the first syllable. For comparison, point out the stress differences in *research* as a noun (**re**search) compared with *research* as a verb (re**search**).

4. Answers for some categories, such as "Can I use world knowledge?" will vary. Some sections of the chart may be completed as follows:

Word or Phrase	Is it important?	Is there an internal definition?	It is a noun? verb? adjective?
1. recently	No (The word does not repeat, and it is not central to the main idea.)	No	Adverb
2. contacts	Yes (The word repeats and it appears in a topic sentence.)	Yes (line 14) *you have to know people* (From the context, we can guess that contacts are people you know in an industry, who can help you to get jobs or other opportunities.)	Noun
3. intern	Yes (The word only appears once, but it is important to the main idea, the description of a process.)	No (But we might guess from the context that an *intern* is like a student, someone who works and learns a job for no or very little pay.)	Noun
4. break	Yes (The word only appears once, but it is important to the main idea, the description of a process.)	No (But we might guess from the context that it means a first or big opportunity.)	Noun
5. seamstress	Yes (The word repeats; it is used in a question and the first line of an answer.)	No (But we can guess from the context, especially line 23 and the *-ess* suffix, that it means a person who can sew.)	Noun
6. depends	Yes (The word is used in the first line of an answer, similar to a topic sentence.)	No	Verb
7. contemporary	Yes (The word is used in an explanation of a main idea.)	No (But we might guess from the contrasting examples of a movie set in the sixties and a "corset movie" set 150 years ago that *contemporary* means modern or present-day.)	Adjective

114 CHAPTER 11

Word or Phrase	Is it important?	Is there an internal definition?	It is a noun? verb? adjective?
8. Academy Award	Yes (The word is used in a question.)	No (But we might guess from the context that it is an important award in the movie industry, and that it can be given to a costume designer.)	Noun

Choices of additional unfamiliar words will vary. Possible unfamiliar, important words: *spotlight, complex, industry, an eye for detail, corsets*.

C. Following Ideas

1. The omitted words that fill in the ellipsis appear in boldface:
   I can sew, but **I can**not **sew** that well.

2. The reference chart should be completed as follows:

Word	Line	Refers to
1. it's	9	the film *Day for Night*
2. it	9	the one day when I saw the film *Day for Night*
3. that	10	the first time I realized how complex and interesting moviemaking was
4. that	24	X (head of a noun clause; no referent)
5. that	31	winning an Academy Award for Costume Design

D. Identifying Main Ideas and Supporting Details

The chart should be completed as follows:

Question	Main Idea	Supporting Details
1. How did you get interested in costume design? Was it a lifelong dream?	I can't say that costume design was a lifelong dream. OR: No, it was not.	**Fact:** I've always been interested in clothes. **Example:** When I was young, my parents owned a clothing store and my first experience with clothing came from working in their shop. **Example:** I studied art in college, and one day I saw the film *Day for Night*, by French director François Truffaut. **Description:** It's the story of the making of a movie. **Fact/Example:** It was the first time I realized how complex and interesting moviemaking was. It looked like fun.
2. Is that when you went to Hollywood?	No. I couldn't go then.	**Fact:** I didn't have any money or contacts. **Fact:** In Hollywood, contacts are important. You have to know people. **Example:** After graduation from college, I got a job in the fashion industry in New York. I worked for several years and saved my money. Then I wrote to several people and offered to work for them for free.
3. You worked for free?	Yes. No one pays you when you go to school, and I was no different than a student.	**Example:** I got a job as an intern in an art department. I did that for a couple of years. **Example:** My first break came when I got a job as a production assistant on *Born on the Fourth of July*. They paid me $200 a week. It wasn't much, but I was on my way.
4. So what does it take to become a costume designer? Do you have to be a good seamstress?	Oh, no! Thank goodness you don't have to be a seamstress.	**Fact:** I can sew, but not that well. **Fact:** Basically, I think that you have to have an eye for detail. **Example:** There are differences in clothing styles that many people might not notice, but they make a difference.

116 CHAPTER 11

Question	Main Idea	Supporting Details
5. Where do you get your ideas?	It depends. If the movie isn't contemporary, you have to do a lot of research to find out about clothes in that time.	**Example:** For example, *Catch Me If You Can* is set in the sixties. I got ideas from lots of places—old fashion magazines, of course, and even old high school yearbooks.
6. So, is your dream to win the Academy Award for Costume Design?	That would be nice, of course. But right now my dream is to work on what I call a "corset" movie . . .	**Description:**—one where the women wear corsets and big dresses like they did 150 years ago.

Remember
Student Book p. 196

Outlines will vary.

Discuss
Student Book p. 196

1. Answers will vary. Possible answers: A costume designer can make a movie better by researching the time period carefully and by creating realistic costumes. The viewers will then feel like they are watching people who are really from that time. A costume designer can make a move worse by creating costumes that are distracting or historically inaccurate.
2. Answers will vary.

Student Book p. 197

Prepare
Student Book p. 197

Answers may vary. Possible answers:
1. Grauman's Chinese Theatre is a theatre in Hollywood where many movie premieres are shown. It is also a place where tourists can see a famous sidewalk of Hollywood stars. (This information can be determined from the title and subtitle, the first and last paragraphs, and the pictures).

2. This article is probably from a magazine and will be read by a general audience of adult and/or teen readers. It does not have very long or complex sentences and it does not have specialized vocabulary.

3. Possible names of famous movie stars who might appear in the text: Marilyn Monroe, Clark Gable, Vivian Leigh, Shirley Temple, Harrison Ford, Tom Hanks, Tom Cruise.

4. Possible additional questions:
   - What Chinese things can you see in the theatre?
   - How much does it cost to visit Grauman's or the sidewalk?

Read
Student Book p. 197

Possible answer to the prediction question from the *Prepare* section:
- Grauman's Chinese Theatre is famous because it has had more movie premieres than any other theatre, and it is next to the famous sidewalk with the impressions of famous Hollywood stars.

Answers to the possible additional prediction questions:
- In the theatre, you can see Chinese decorations (a red pagoda and a dragon) and exhibits of Chinese artifacts. However, the theatre isn't really Chinese, and it doesn't show Chinese films.

CHAPTER 11 **117**

- Both Grauman's and the sidewalk can be visited for free.

Read Again
Student Book p. 198

Practice of individual reading strategies should be encouraged; answers will vary.

The main idea of each paragraph should be identified as follows:

Paragraph 1: Every movie lover who visits Hollywood should visit Grauman's Chinese Theatre.

Paragraph 2: (The main idea is implied, not stated directly in a topic sentence): Grauman's Chinese Theatre is mostly famous for its movie premieres.

Paragraph 3: However, most people don't go to Grauman's Chinese Theatre to see a movie. They go to look at the sidewalk.

Paragraph 4: Many of them (visitors) compare their feet with the stars' feet.

Paragraph 5: In addition to the handprints, footprints, and signatures, you'll discover that some of the stars left some other things.

Paragraph 6: Another amazing thing about Grauman's is the cost to tour it.

For connectors and their referents, see *C. Following Ideas* on TM page 119.

Signal words and predictions:

- *And* (lines 3, 5, 8, 21, 23, 27-30, 37, 47, 49-50) indicates additional information.
- *Such as* (lines 5, 22, 25) indicates an example.
- *However* (lines 5, 18, 34) indicates contrasting information.
- *In 1927* (lines 10-11) indicates time or chronology of events.
- *Also* (lines 11, 46) indicates additional information.
- *First* (lines 12, 13) indicates time, chronology of events.
- *Since then* (line 14) indicates time or chronology of events.
- *Because of* (line 15) indicates a reason or cause.
- *From 1973 to 2000* (line 17) indicates time.
- *But* (line 24) indicates contrasting information.
- *In recent years* (lines 24-25) indicates time.
- *In addition* (line 37) indicates additional information.
- *In 1995* (lines 49) indicates time or chronology of events.
- *Another* (line 51) indicates additional information.

Post-Reading Activities

A. Comprehension Check

1. The theatre is called Grauman's Chinese Theatre after Sid Grauman, the man who opened it.
2. The theatre opened in 1927.
3. The theatre is famous because it has had more movie premieres than any other theatre, and it is next to the famous sidewalk with the impressions of famous Hollywood stars.
4. More than 2 million people a year visit the theatre.
5. Many tourists like to visit the sidewalk outside the theatre.
6. In the cement, you can find imprints of things from famous movie stars: signatures, handprints, footprints, and even noseprints, legprints, braided hair, and horse hoofprints.

B. Vocabulary Check

1. *Handprint, footprint, hoofprint,* and *imprint* are all related; the first three are examples of imprints. Also, all words except for *imprint* are compound nouns.

   a. handprint = the print or impression of a hand
   b. footprint = the print or impression of a foot
   c. hoofprint = the print or impression of an animal hoof
   d. imprint = an impression of something

2. Answers for some categories, such as "Can I use world knowledge?" will vary. Some sections of the chart may be completed as follows:

Word	Is it important?	Is there an internal definition?	It is a noun? verb? adjective?
1. pagoda	Yes (The word appears in the title and in the first paragraph.)	No (But from the context we might guess that it is some kind of Chinese style of building.)	Noun
2. dragon	No (The word appears only once, and it is part of a description; it is not really central to the main idea of the article.) **OR:** Yes (The word appears in the first paragraph.)	No (But from the context we might guess that it is some kind of Chinese design, maybe an animal.)	Noun
3. artifacts	No (The word appears only once, and it is part of a description; it is not really central to the main idea of the article.) **OR:** Yes (The word appears in the first paragraph.)	Yes (line 5) Examples: *such as clothing, paintings, and weapons. Artifacts* is the group or class of which these things are examples.	Noun
4. weapons	No (The word appears only once, and it is part of a description; it is not really central to the main idea of the article.) **OR:** Yes (the word appears in the first paragraph, and it is part of a definition.)	Yes (lines 4–5) The word can be defined by looking at the other examples: *Chinese artifacts such as clothing, paintings, and weapons. Artifacts* is the group or class of which these things are examples. *Weapons* is an example of an artifact.	Noun

Word	Is it important?	Is there an internal definition?	It is a noun? verb? adjective?
5. fooled	No (The word appears in the first paragraph, but the main idea can be understood without knowing this word.)	No (But we might guess from the context that it means *deceived* or *misled*.)	Verb (Here it may appear to be an adjective—there is a past participle *-ed* ending and it follows the *be* verb; however, it is really a verb in the passive voice.)
6. premiere	Yes (The word repeats.)	Yes (line 13) *premiere, or first showing*	Noun
7. cement	Yes (The word repeats.)	Yes (line 20) Related word: *sidewalk*—a sidewalk is made of cement	Noun
8. autographs	Yes (The word repeats with a synonym, and is closely related to the main idea.)	Yes (line 38) Synonym: *signatures*	Noun
9. performers	Yes (The word repeats with a synonym.)	Yes (lines 21–22 and line 24) Related words: *movie stars, stars*	Noun
10. signatures	Yes (The word repeats with a synonym, and is closely related to the main idea.)	Yes (line 21) Synonym: *autographs*	Noun
11. impressions	Yes (The word repeats and is closely related to the main idea.)	Yes (lines 40, 44) Synonym: *imprint*; (lines 27–28) Explanation of the process in this context: *put their hands and feet in the wet cement*	Noun

Choices of additional unfamiliar words will vary. Possible unfamiliar, important words: *tradition, exhibits, ownership, characters, compare, cigar, cowboy, braids, amazing*.

C. Following Ideas

The omitted words that fill in the ellipsis appear in boldface:

1. Inside **Grauman's Chinese Theatre**, there are exhibits of Chinese artifacts.
2. There is a cement impression of Jimmy Durante's nose and **a cement impression** of Bob Hope's nose.

D. Predicting Ideas with Signal Words

The paragraph should be rewritten with the sentences in the following order:

    More than two million people a year visit Grauman's Chinese Theatre. Many of them compare their feet with the stars'. However, few are as small as Jeanette MacDonald's, a star of the 1920s and 30s. Her footprint is just 6 1/2 inches long! In addition to the handprints, footprints, and signatures, you'll discover that some of the stars left other things.

E. Identifying Main Ideas and Supporting Details

The chart should be completed as follows:

Paragraph	Main Idea	Supporting Details
1	Every movie lover who visits Hollywood should visit Grauman's Chinese Theatre.	**Description:** The theatre looks like a giant red pagoda, and there is a huge dragon in the front. Inside there are exhibits of Chinese artifacts such as clothing, paintings, and weapons. **Facts:** Grauman's Chinese Theatre isn't really Chinese. It wasn't built by a Chinese American, and it doesn't show Chinese movies.
2	(The main idea is implied, not stated directly in a topic sentence): Grauman's Chinese Theatre is famous mostly for its movie premieres.	**Facts:** Sid Grauman opened the Chinese Theatre in 1927. He also built the nearby Egyptian Theatre. The first movie the Chinese Theatre showed was the premiere, or first showing, of the silent film *King of Kings*. Since then, the Chinese Theatre has had more movie premieres than any other theatre. (Because of a change in ownership, the theatre was known as Mann's Chinese Theatre from 1973 to 2000.)
3	However, most people don't go to Grauman's Chinese Theatre to see a movie. They go to look at the sidewalk.	**Statistic:** There in the cement are the footprints, handprints, and autographs of more than 200 movie stars. **Facts/Examples:** These include stars from the past such as Marilyn Monroe, Elizabeth Taylor, Clark Gable, and John Wayne. In recent years, popular performers such as Meryl Streep, Whoopi Goldberg, Tom Hanks, Arnold Schwarzenegger, Harrison Ford, and Tom Cruise put their hands and feet in the wet cement. Directors Steven Spielberg and George Lucas and the *Star Wars* characters of Darth Vadar, R2D2, and C-3PO did, too.
4	Many of them (visitors) compare their feet with the stars'.	**Statistic:** More than 2 million people a year visit Grauman's Chinese Theatre. **Fact:** Few are as small as Jeanette Mac Donald's, a star of the 1920's and 30s. **Fact:** Her footprint is just 6 1/2 inches long!

Paragraph	Main Idea	Supporting Details
5	In addition to the handprints, footprints, and signatures, you'll discover that some of the stars left some other things.	**Examples:** Comedian Groucho Marx left an imprint of his cigar; Cowboy actor Roy Rogers's horse Trigger left his hoofprints; 1940s movie star Betty Grable left an imprint of her famous legs; There are also cement impressions of two famous noses: Jimmy Durante's and Bob Hope's; And in 1995, Whoopie Goldberg cut off her braids and made an imprint of them in the wet cement!
6	Another amazing thing about Grauman's is the cost to tour it.	**Facts:** The courtyard is free of charge to all visitors. You do not even have to buy at ticket at the theatre to find the impressions of your favorite stars.

Remember
Student Book p. 200

Outlines may vary. Possible outline:

Grauman's Chinese Theatre—A Hollywood Tradition

I. Grauman's Chinese Theatre
   A. What it looks like
      1. red pagoda
      2. huge dragon in front
      3. exhibits of Chinese artifacts such as clothing, painting, and weapons
   B. Why it's not really Chinese
      1. was opened by Sid Grauman, not by a Chinese man
      2. hows Hollywood movie premieres, not Chinese movies
   C. History of Grauman's
      1. opened in 1927 (by Sid Grauman)
      2. first movie premiere: *King of Kings* (silent film)
      3. change of ownership; theatre was called Mann's Chinese Theatre from1973 to 2000
   D. Visiting Grauman's
      1. most people come to see the sidewalk, not movies
      2. admission is free
      3. no ticket is needed

II. The Sidewalk
   A. Has footprints, handprints, and autographs of more than 200 movie stars
      1. stars from the past
         a. Marilyn Monroe
         b. Elizabeth Taylor
         c. Clark Gable
         d. John Wayne
      2. stars from the present
         a. Meryl Streep
         b. Whoopi Goldberg
         c. Tom Hanks
         d. Arnold Schwarzenegger
         e. Harrison Ford
         f. Tom Cruise
   B. Has impressions of famous directors
      1. Steven Spielberg
      2. George Lucas
   C. Has impressions of famous film characters from movies like *Star Wars*
      1. Darth Vader
      2. R2D2
      3. C-3P0
   D. Also has other kinds of impressions
      1. Groucho Marx's cigar
      2. Roy Rogers's horse Trigger's hoofprints
      3. Betty Grable's legs
      4. noses
         a. Jimmy Durante
         b. Bob Hope
      5. Whoopi Goldberg's braids

Discuss
Student Book p. 200

Answers will vary.

CHAPTER 12

Reading: Bridges

Getting Started
Student Book p. 202

1. Answers will vary.
2. Answers will vary.
3. Answers may vary. Possible answers: This chapter may talk about how bridges are built. It may talk about famous bridges—bridges that are landmarks or that were important in history. It may talk about dangers or accidents involving bridges.

Prepare
Student Book p. 203

Answers may vary. Possible answers:

1. The topic of this reading is a bridge called London Bridge, and it is located in Arizona, in the United States, not in London, England. After skimming the first and last paragraphs, it seems that the actual London Bridge was moved by a businessman from England to Arizona, and that now it is a popular tourist attraction.
2. The reading is a newspaper article. There is a headline, a city and state in the first paragraph, no author, and a photograph. The sentences do not seem long or complex, and there is no specialized or complex vocabulary. There are no charts or graphs. The article seems to be written for general readers. The purpose may be to inform readers about the history of the bridge; there are many dates given in the article and many time phrases in the topic sentences.
3. The main idea seems to be that the London Bridge was moved from England to Arizona, and that it is now a tourist attraction.
4. Pre-reading questions will vary. Possible questions:

   - Why is the London Bridge in Arizona?
   - Who decided to move the bridge?
   - How was the bridge moved?

Read
Student Book p. 203

Answers to the possible prediction questions from the *Prepare* section:

- The London Bridge was having troubles in the 1960s, and English officials wanted to build a new one. A businessman decided to buy the bridge and move it to Arizona as a tourist attraction.
- A businessman named Robert McCulloch decided to move the bridge.
- The bridge was moved by workers who took apart the bridge and numbered the bricks. The bricks were shipped to Los Angeles and then taken to Arizona in trucks. The bricks were then put together again according to the numbers.

Read Again
Student Book p. 203

Practice of individual reading strategies should be encouraged; answers will vary.

For the main idea of each paragraph, see *E. Identifying Main Ideas and Supporting Details* on TM page 125.

For connectors and signal words, see *C. Following Ideas* and *D. Predicting Ideas with Signal Words* on TM page 125.

Post-Reading Activities

A. Comprehension Check

1. a. $2.4 million = the price that McCulloch and a friend paid for the London Bridge—and the highest price ever paid for an antique
   b. 1968 = the year that workers began disassembling the bridge in London

122

c. KBBC = the local radio station in Lake Havasu City, Arizona (also known as BBC radio)

d. $7 million = the cost of moving the bridge from London to Arizona

e. 10,000 = the number of miles the bricks traveled by ship from London to Los Angeles

f. 1971 = the year that the bridge was finally ready (completely rebuilt in Arizona)

g. 45,000 = the population of Lake Havasu City

2. The "crazy dream of an Arizona businessman" was the dream of buying the London Bridge and moving it to Arizona.

3. People thought McCulloch was crazy because the community where he wanted to put it was close to a manmade lake, they didn't see how a bridge could be moved around the world, and they thought an English bridge would look ridiculous in the Arizona desert.

4. The British wanted to sell London Bridge because it was being damaged by heavy modern cars, trucks, and buses, and it was sinking into the Thames River.

5. Workers numbered the bridge's bricks so that the bridge could be rebuilt according to a numbered diagram.

B. **Vocabulary Check**

1. To disassemble something is to take it apart; to reassemble something is to put it together again. (Students should note the prefixes *dis-* and *re-*.)

2. *Manmade* = made by man, by humans (not natural); *double-decker* = a bus with two decks, or two levels

3. One abbreviation: *Ariz.* (line 1) = Arizona; one acronym (similar to an abbreviation): *BBC* = British Broadcasting Company

4. Answers for some categories, such as "Can I use world knowledge?" will vary. Some sections of the chart may be completed as follows:

Word	Is it important?	Is there an internal definition?	It is a noun? verb? adjective?
1. crazy	Yes (The word is a description word, but it repeats, and it is used in the first and last paragraphs.)	Yes (line 8) Related word: *ridiculous* (Also, from the context we might guess that it means strange or unrealistic.)	Adjective
2. ridiculous	Yes (The word is a description word, but it is used in the first paragraph and relates to the main idea of the paragraph.)	Yes (line 2) Related word: *crazy* (Also, from the context we might guess that it means strange, unusual, or out of place.)	Adjective
3. sinking	Yes (The word relates to the main idea of the paragraph.)	No (But from the context, we might guess that it means being pushed down because of weight; in lines 12–13, we are told that the cars on the bridge are too *heavy*.)	Verb

Word	Is it important?	Is there an internal definition?	It is a noun? verb? adjective?
4. numbered	Yes (The word repeats.)	No (But from the context we might guess that it means to put numbers on things, or to label with numbers.)	Verb (line 21) Adjective (line 26)
5. bricks	Yes (The word repeats.)	No (But from the context we can understand that *bricks* are a type of building material; the bridge was made of individual bricks.)	Noun
6. attract	Yes (The word appears in topic sentence, and it repeats in a different form.)	No (But from the context we can guess that it means making people want to come see something; understanding the noun *attraction* as a place that tourists want to see, helps us to understand the verb.)	Verb
7. authentic	Yes (The word is a description word, but it relates to the main idea of the paragraph.)	No (But from the context we might guess that it means realistic; also, the word *typical*, line 33, is related.)	Adjective
8. typical	Yes (The word is a description word, but it relates to the main idea of the paragraph.)	No (But from the context we might guess that it means realistic; also, the word *authentic*, line 31, is related.)	Adjective
9. pubs	Yes (The word relates to the main idea of the paragraph; it is an example that can help us understand the main idea.)	No (But we might guess from context that they are places, like *shops*, line 33, that people can go to.)	Noun

Choices of additional unfamiliar words will vary. Possible unfamiliar, important words: *community, desert, refused, trucks, officials, antique, diagram, village.*

C. Following Ideas

The reference chart should be completed as follows:

Word or Phrase	Line	Refers to
1. that	16	London officials wanted to build a new bridge, but they didn't know what to do with the old one. **OR:** the early 1960s
2. them	22	the bricks
3. that point	23	the time when the bricks arrived in Los Angeles (Note: this point in time must be inferred; there is no word or phrase that serves as a direct antecedent.)

D. Predicting Ideas with Signal Words

Signal Word — **Purpose**

First of all (line 4) — to show the order of information

Second (line 6) — to show the order of information

Third (line 7) — to show the order of information

But (line 9) — to show contrasting information

E. Identifying Main Ideas and Supporting Details

Paragraph	Main Idea	Supporting Details
1	People thought that Robert McCulloch was crazy when he decided to buy the London Bridge and move it to Arizona.	**Facts:** The community where he wanted to put it was close to a manmade lake, they didn't see how a bridge could be moved around the world, and they thought an English bridge would look ridiculous in the Arizona desert.
2	In the early 1960s, the London Bridge was in trouble.	**Facts:** Modern cars, trucks, and buses were too heavy, and the bridge was sinking into the Thames River. London officials wanted to build a new bridge, but they didn't know what to do with the old one. **Fact:** That was when McCulloch and a friend offered to buy it. It cost them $2.4 million. **Statistic:** At the time, it was the highest price ever paid for an antique.

126 CHAPTER 12

Paragraph	Main Idea	Supporting Details
3	Workers then began disassembling the bridge in London in 1968.	**Example (OR description of a process):** They numbered the bricks before they put them on boats and sent them 10,000 miles to Los Angeles. At that point, they were put on trucks and taken to Arizona. Workers in the Arizona desert then reassembled the bricks according to a numbered diagram. **Facts:** Moving the bridge cost $7 million, but the bridge was finally ready in 1971.
4	However, McCulloch knew that he needed more than a famous bridge to attract people to Lake Havasu City, so he created an authentic English village next to the bridge.	**Description:** The village has typical English shops and pubs. Visitors can even ride on a double-decker bus and listen to the local radio station KBBC, known as BBC radio.
5	Today, the London Bridge is one of Arizona's biggest attractions, and Lake Havasu City is a lively town of 45,000—all because of the crazy dream of an Arizona businessman.	No supporting details-paragraph is one sentence only. However, a statistic is used in the sentence (population *45,000*).

Remember
Student Book p. 207

Outlines may vary. Possible outline:

Moving the London Bridge to Arizona
  I. Disassembling the Bridge
   A. Work started in 1968
   B. Workers numbered the bricks
   C. The bricks were shipped by boat 10,000 miles to Los Angeles
   D. The bricks were taken to Arizona on trucks
  II. Reassembling the Bridge
   A. Workers in the Arizona desert used a numbered diagram to put the bricks together
   B. The bridge was rebuilt by 1971

Discuss
Student Book p. 207

1. Answers will vary. Possible answers: No, countries should not sell their important landmarks because they are a part of that culture's history and culture. The landmarks should stay in the country so that future generations can see them and learn about them. Landmarks should not be for sale—they are part of the land that they come from!
(OR) Yes, countries should sell their important landmarks if they want to. The money raised from the sale could be used to improve other landmarks or to create new ones. Many countries need money more than they need the landmarks. The landmarks can be preserved in photographs and films; selling, moving, or even destroying the landmark does not mean that it never existed. Some landmarks have unpleasant memories for many people, and it is good to move them andto sell them—for example, when the Berlin Wall came down, it was destroyed, and pieces of it were sold.

2. Answers will vary.

CHAPTER 12 **127**

Prepare
Student Book p. 207

Answers may vary. Possible answers:
1. A text like this would probably be found in a textbook. It might be used for a class in civil engineering or construction.
2. The text may be somewhat difficult to read. It is long, and it contains many new or specialized vocabulary words. However, it includes definitions and illustrations (diagrams). It seems to be written for learners, not for experts, so its purpose will be to make the meaning of the main ideas and terms clear.
3. Possible ideas/terms related to bridges: *wires, cables, feet, meters, support, weight, pressure.*
4. Pre-reading questions will vary. Possible questions:
   - What types of bridges are there?
   - Which bridge is the best for long distances?
   - Which bridge is the best for short distances?

Read
Student Book p. 207

Answers to the possible prediction questions from the *Prepare* section:
- There are three main types of bridges: beam bridges, arch bridges, and suspension bridges.
- Suspension bridges are best for long distances.
- Beam bridges are best for short distances.

Read Again
Student Book p. 209

Practice of individual reading strategies should be encouraged; answers will vary.

For connectors and signal words, see *C. Following Ideas* and *D. Predicting Ideas with Signal Words* on TM page 129.

Post-Reading Activities

A. Comprehension Check

The chart should be completed as follows:

Characteristic	Beam Bridge	Arch Bridge	Suspension Bridge
1. It can span long distances.			X
2. It is the simplest bridge.	X		
3. It has cables and towers.			X
4. It dissipates tension and compression.		X	
5. Romans built many of these.		X	

B. Vocabulary Check

1. a. *compress* (v) = compression (n)
   b. *short* (adj) = shorten (v)
   c. *length* (n) = lengthen (v)
   d. *dissipate* (v) = dissipation (n)
   e. *transfer* (v) = transference (n)

2. Answers for some categories, such as "Can I use world knowledge?" will vary. Some sections of the chart may be completed as follows:

Word	Is it important?	Is there an internal definition?	It is a noun? verb? adjective?
1. span	Yes (The word repeats.)	Yes (lines 2–3) *the distance between two bridge supports such as columns, towers or the wall of a canyon*	Noun and verb
2. support	Yes (The word repeats.)	Yes (line 3) Examples: *bridge supports such as columns, towers, or the wall of a canyon*; we can infer that supports are things that hold up a bridge	Noun and verb
3. tension	Yes (The word repeats and it is defined.)	Yes (lines 13–14) *Tension is a force that acts to expand or lengthen the thing it is acting on.*	Noun
4. spring	Yes (The word repeats and it is used as an example to define another key term.)	No	Noun
5. buckle	Yes (The word repeats in different forms.)	Yes (lines 20–21) *When there is too much compression, a bridge buckles.* We might infer from this that a bridge breaks, or snaps in two, when it *buckles*.	Verb
6. snap	Yes (The word repeats.)	Yes (line 21) *When there is too much tension, it (the bridge) snaps.* We might infer that the bridge breaks.	Verb
7. concentrated	Yes (The word is part of an explanation of a key word/concept.)	Yes (lines 22–23) Opposite idea/word: *To dissipate force is to spread it out. In this way, the force is not concentrated in one spot.*	Adjective
8. weakness	Yes (The word is part of an explanation of a key word/concept.)	Yes (line 24) Antonym: *strength*	Noun

Choices of additional unfamiliar words will vary. Possible unfamiliar, important words: *cross, canyon, sophisticated, forces, ordinary, press down on, present.*

C. Following Ideas

The omitted words that fill in the ellipsis appear in boldface: Why can an arch bridge span greater distances than a beam bridge **can**, or **why can** a suspension bridge **span distances** seven times as much as an arch bridge **can**?

D. Predicting Ideas with Signal Words

1. a. for example = line 4
   b. in other words = line 16
   c. while = line 4
2. Possible restatements of ideas following each signal word:
   a. A beam bridge today can go across a distance of up to 200 feet.
   b. In other words, we push on both ends (or squeeze it together).
   c. An arch bridge today can cross a distance of 800 or 1,000 feet.
3. Predictions of ideas that came before each signal word may vary. Possible predictions:
   a. The biggest difference between bridges is the distance they can cross.
   b. We compress something when we exert pressure from two opposing sides.
   c. A beam bridge is ideal for shorter spans of up to 200 feet.

E. Identifying Main Ideas and Supporting Details

The chart could be completed as follows:

Section Topic	Main Idea	Supporting Details
Types of bridges (lines 1–6)	There are three basic types of bridges: beam bridges, arch bridges, and suspension bridges. The biggest difference between the three is the distances they can cross in a single span.	**Facts:** A modern beam bridge can span a distance of up to 200 feet. A modern arch bridge can span up to 800 or 1,000 feet. A suspension bridge can span up to 7,000 feet.
Why bridges can span certain distances (lines 7–18) (**OR:** compression and tension)	Bridges can span different distances because of two forces: compression and tension.	**Example:** An ordinary spring is a good example of compression and tension. When we press down on a spring, we push the two ends of the spring together. In other words, we compress it. The force of the compression shortens the spring. When we pull the two ends of the spring apart, we create tension in the spring. The force of the tension lengthens the spring.
How compression and tension are used in all bridges (lines 19-25) (**OR:** dissipation and transference)	The forces of compression and tension are used in all bridges.	**Fact:** The design of the bridge must be able to control these forces without buckling or snapping. **Fact:** When there is too much compression, a bridge buckles. When there is too much tension, it snaps. The best way to control these forces is to dissipate them or transfer them. **Example:** An arch bridge is a good example of dissipation. **Example:** A suspension bridge is a good example of transference.

Remember
Student Book p. 211

Description of outlines may vary. Possible description of an outline:

> The name of each type of bridge might start on the left.
>
> Information about span might be indented beneath each bridge type.
>
> Information about how compression and tension are dissipated or transferred could be further indented under each bridge type.

Discuss
Student Book p. 211

Answers may vary. Possible answers:

1. The best kind of bridge for each place might be as follows:
   a. A suspension bridge is best for a 4,000-foot span across an ocean bay because a suspension bridge has the largest span of all bridges. It is the most sophisticated bridge type, and this is a long distance to cross.
   b. An arch bridge is best for a 120-foot span across a highway. The arch bridge is good for a span of this distance. Romans often built arch bridges over roads and highways. A beam bridge might also work, since it can span distances of up to 200 feet.
   c. Either an arch bridge or a suspension bridge could be used for a 700-foot span across a deep canyon gorge. A beam bridge would not be strong enough for such a wide span.
2. Answers will vary. Possible answers: Some famous bridges in other countries include the Pont d'Avignon (France), the Ponte Vecchio (Italy), the Akashi Kaikyo Bridge (Japan).

Prepare
Student Book p. 212

Answers may vary. Possible answers:
1. The purpose of this encyclopedia entry is to inform readers about the longest suspension bridge in the world and to give information about its basic features. It will also compare this bridge to other long suspension bridges in the world.
2. The best methods to use to read the text include skimming the first paragraph, scanning the table, reading the headings/subtitles, and studying the photo on page 202 of the Student Book.
3. Possible terms related to bridges and statistics: *meters, feet, size, strength, diameter, measure, weight, height.*
4. The text will probably not explain why the Akashi Kaikyo Bridge was built. The information seems to be mostly about statistics —how long the bridge took to plan and to build, how long it is compared to other bridges, how high it is, and how strong it is.

Read
Student Book p. 212

The text does not explain why the Akashi Kaikyo Bridge was built, for the reasons stated in #4 of the *Prepare* section.

Read Again
Student Book p. 212

Practice of individual reading strategies should be encouraged; answers will vary.

Types of facts that should be noted include statistics and examples of/on: location, time spent planning and building, age, length, height, diameter, size of anchorage, strength.

For signal words, see *C. Predicting Ideas with Signal Words* on TM page 132.

Post-Reading Activities

A. Comprehension Check

1. The second longest suspension bridge in the world is the Great Belt East Bridge in Denmark.
2. The oldest of the ten bridges is the Golden Gate Bridge in the U.S.
3. The Hoga Kusten Bridge is in Sweden.
4. The Great Belt East Bridge is longer than the Golden Gate Bridge.
5. Piano wire was used to form the suspension cables of the Akashi Bridge.

6. 350,000 tons of concrete were used to anchor the Akashi.
7. The Akashi Kaikyo Bridge can survive an earthquake that measures up to 8.5 on the Richter scale.

B. Vocabulary Check

1. a. *long* (adj) = length (n)
   b. *high* (adj) = height (n)
   c. *deep* (adj) = depth (n)
2. Three abbreviations and their meanings: *m* (meters), *mm* (millimeters), *sec* (seconds).
3. Answers for some categories, such as "Can I use world knowledge?" will vary. Some sections of the chart may be completed as follows:

Word	Is it important?	Is there an internal definition?	It is a noun? verb? adjective?
1. diameter	Yes (The word appears in a heading and it repeats.)	No	Noun
2. wire	Yes (The word repeats.)	No (But we might infer from the context that it is something that goes into the making of a cable, a material that is long, thin, and strong.)	Noun
3. strands	Yes (The word is part of a definition of a key term.)	No (But we might infer from the context that *strands* are small pieces of something—here, the strands are individual pieces of wire, which in turn go into cables.)	Noun
4. anchorage	Yes (The word appears in a heading and it repeats.)	No (But we might infer from the context that it has to do with the ends of the bridges, holding the ends into the ground with concrete.)	Noun
5. tons	No (It is enough to know that the term refers to a measurement.)	No (But we may infer from the context that it is a unit of measurement, referring to a large quantity.)	Noun
6. withstand	Yes (The word is used in an example that helps to define a key concept.)	No (But we might infer from the context that it means to *resist* or *survive*.)	Verb

Choices of additional unfamiliar words will vary. Possible unfamiliar, important words: *rank, foundations, concrete, survive, earthquake, Richter scale*.

C. Predicting Ideas with Signal Words

1. The main method that connects the text's main points is numbered lists. (There are numbered items in the chart and after the chart).
2. Words that could substitute for signal words in the chart: *First, second, next, third,* etc. Signal words that could be used in the beginning and end of the reading: *also, additionally, in addition to, another.*

Remember
Student Book p. 214

Picture notes will vary. Students may label the following features on their picture of the Akashi Bridge: towers (with height of 300 m), suspension cables, anchorage (one foundation on each end, 63.5 m deep). Pictures might also show the bridge on a map, crossing over water labeled the Akashi Straits. The bridge connects Maiko, Tarumi Ward in Kobe City to Matsuho, Awaji-cho, Tsuna-gun, on Awaji Island.

Discuss
Student Book p. 214

1. Answers may vary. Possible answers: Before bridges were built, people probably crossed water by boat (ferries, canoes, etc.) or, if the water was not too wide or too dangerous, on horseback or by swimming. In some cases, people may not have been able to cross water at all without a bridge; therefore, the land they wanted to get to would have been inaccessible, or they would have had to travel by land to find an alternate route.
2. Answers may vary. Possible answers: Big dangers to bridges include earthquakes, excessive weight, and high winds (especially for bridges with suspension cables).

Prepare
Student Book p. 215

Answers may vary. Possible answers:

1. The photos show the four stages of a bridge collapsing (breaking/buckling).
2. The article's purpose is to inform readers about a famous bridge collapse, a disaster involving a suspension bridge. This news story is not recent; it was written on November 7, 1960.
3. Brainstorming what happens during a bridge disaster depends on the type of bridge and the type of disaster: high winds could cause suspension bridge cables to snap; excess weight could cause a bridge to buckle.
4. Pre-reading questions will vary. Possible questions:
   - Where was this bridge?
   - When did this disaster happen?
   - Why did the bridge break? (What caused the bridge to break?)

Read
Student Book p. 215

Answers to the possible prediction questions from the *Prepare* section:

- This bridge was located near the city of Tacoma in Washington State.
- This disaster occurred on November 7, 1940, at 11:00 A.M.
- The bridge broke during a high wind. It moved so much that a support cable in the center broke. Also, a support bracket on the center span slipped and caused the center cables to loosen. As a result, the bridge not only moved up and down, it also twisted around. It's possible that the use of light steel in the bridge's construction was a factor.

Read Again
Student Book p. 216

Practice of individual reading strategies should be encouraged; answers will vary.

The main idea of each paragraph should be identified as follows:

Paragraph 1: Twenty years ago today, at 11:00 A.M., the Tacoma Narrows suspension bridge collapsed.
Possible restatement: One morning two decades ago, the Tacoma Narrows suspension bridge buckled.

Paragraph 2: According to design experts, there were several possible reasons for the bridge failure.
Possible restatement: Design specialists believed there were many reasons the bridge collapsed.

Paragraph 3: This (the use of steel) proved to be a tragic mistake.
Possible restatement: This was a terrible error.

Paragraph 4: Architects and engineers remember the disaster.
Possible restatement: Designers of the bridge recall the tragedy.

Paragraph 5: In 1950, a new $18 million bridge opened on the site of the first Tacoma Narrows Bridge.
Possible restatement: A new bridge, costing nearly $20 million, was constructed in place of Galloping Gertie ten years later.

For connectors and signal words, see *C. Following Ideas* and *D. Predicting Ideas with Signal Words* on TM page 135.

Post-Reading Activities

A. Comprehension Check

1. The Tacoma Narrows Bridge was only a few months old when it collapsed.
2. The bridge was famous because it moved a lot during high winds—it was nicknamed "Galloping Gertie."
3. The engineers made the mistake of using light steel. Light steel was used a lot at that time to build bridges with lighter loads.
4. When the wind blew, the bridge moved up and down and it also twisted around from side to side.
5. As a result of this disaster, engineers today predict how a bridge will behave in strong winds. To do this, they use wind tunnel tests and mathematical models. They design bridges to resist twisting forces and to control movement.
6. The bridge is designed to resist torsional (twisting) forces and special dampers at the ends control movement on the newer Tacoma Narrows Bridge.

B. Vocabulary Check

1. T 2. F 3. T 4. F 5. T

6. Answers for some categories, such as "Can I use world knowledge?" will vary. Some sections of the chart may be completed as follows:

Word	Is it important?	Is there an internal definition?	It is a noun? verb? adjective?
1. collapse	Yes (The word repeats and it is in the title.)	Yes (line 10) Synonym: *broke*	Noun (title); Verb (line 3)
2. movement	Yes (The word repeats, in different forms.)	Yes (line 29) Synonym: *motions*, also the word is used as a verb, *move*, throughout the article, and we learn how it moves: *up and down* and *twisting*.	Noun
3. violently	Yes (The word repeats, in a different form—*violent*, adjective)	Yes (line 6) Synonym: *wild*	Adverb

Word	Is it important?	Is there an internal definition?	It is a noun? verb? adjective?
4. unbalanced	Yes (It's a description word, but it helps to explain a key part of the process and therefore relates to the main idea.)	Yes (line 16) Antonym: *stable* (Also, we can guess from the prefix *un–* that it means *not balanced*.)	Adjective
5. stable	Yes (It is a description word, but it helps to explain a key part of the process and therefore relates to the main idea.)	Yes (line 10 Antonym: *unbalanced*	Adjective
6. bracket	Yes (It helps to explain a key part of the process and therefore relates to the main idea.)	No (But we can guess from the context that this is part of the bridge's support system.)	Noun
7. loosen	Yes (It helps to explain a key part of the process and therefore relates to the main idea.)	No (But we can guess from another form of the word, *loose* that this word may mean to cause something to come loose.)	Verb
8. wild	Yes (The word is a description word and is used only once, but it appears in the first paragraph and relates to the main idea of the paragraph.)	Yes (lines 9 and 29) Synonyms: *violently, violent*	Adjective
9. dampers	No (The word is a specialized term for a new design on the bridge, and could be important; however, the main idea of the paragraph is that the new bridge has safer designs; the meaning is clear without more specific knowledge of this term.)	No (But we might infer that it is something attached to each end of a bridge.)	Noun

Word	Is it important?	Is there an internal definition?	It is a noun? verb? adjective?
10. lighter	Yes (It helps to explain a key part of the process and therefore relates to the main idea.)	Yes (line 14) Antonym: *stronger*	Adjective (comparative)
11. aerodynamics	Yes (It helps provide support for the main idea of the paragraph.)	Yes (lines 36–37) Restatement: *...we had to find a way to predict how a bridge will behave in strong winds*	Noun

Choices of additional unfamiliar words will vary. Possible unfamiliar, important words: *galloping, nickname, load, failure, steel, tragic, slipped, twisting, blow, break up, plunged, disaster, tunnel, site.*

C. Following Ideas

The reference chart should be completed as follows:

Word or Phrase	Line	Refers to
1. that	5	only a few months old
2. this	10	a support cable in the center of the bridge broke
3. these bridges	19	many more bridges were built in 1940
4. this	23	The Tacoma Narrows bridge was built using light steel.

D. Predicting Ideas with Signal Words

1. **a.** cause = due to (line 17)
   = because (line 19)
   = caused (lines 28, 29)
   = in turn (line 29)
   b. contrast = however (lines 19, 25)
   c. effect = hence (line 7)
   = so (line 16)
   d. time and sequence = Twenty years ago today (line 1)
   = at 11:00 A.M. (lines 1–2)
   = On November 7, 1940 (line 8)
   = after that terrible disaster (line 36)
   = In 1950 (line 40)

2. effect signal word in paragraph 2 = *so* (line 16)
   effect signal word in paragraph 3 = *in turn* (line 29)

136 CHAPTER 12

E. Identifying Main Ideas and Supporting Details

Paragraph	Main Idea	Supporting Details
1	Twenty years ago today, at 11:00 A.M., the Tacoma Narrows suspension bridge collapsed.	**Facts:** The bridge had become known for its wild movements during high winds. The bridge was known as "Galloping Gertie." On November 7, 1940, it moved so violently that a support cable broke. This broken cable created an unbalanced load that caused the bridge to collapse.
2	There were several possible reasons for the bridge failure.	**Facts:** Steel is commonly used to make bridges stronger, and the weight of steel makes most bridges stable, so engineers at the time didn't worry about wind. Due to an increase in traffic, many bridges were built in 1940. However, because these bridges had lighter loads, engineers built lighter bridges. The Tacoma Narrows Bridge was built using light steel.
3	This (using light steel to build the bridge) was a tragic mistake.	**Facts:** The winds in Puget Sound were strong and made the bridge move up and down. A support bracket on the center span slipped and caused the center cables to loosen. This loosening caused the bridge to twist violently in the wind. The bridge began to break up. Commuters plunged to their deaths in the water.

F. Making Inferences

Two possible inferences that can be made from the passage:

- Bridges today are stronger and safer because of what architects and engineers learned from the Tacoma Narrows Bridge disaster.
- One possible reason for the bridge collapse was that architects and engineers didn't really understand the importance of aerodynamics. (And therefore, architects and engineers might be partially responsible for the disaster).

Remember
Student Book p. 218

Choice of graphic organizer may vary. A logical graphic organizer to show the collapse of Gertie would be a block diagram. A timeline might also work. Possible block diagram:

By 1940, railroad and automobile traffic had increased.

Engineers were building lighter bridges, out of light steel.

Engineers built the Tacoma Narrows Bridge using light steel.

CHAPTER 12   137

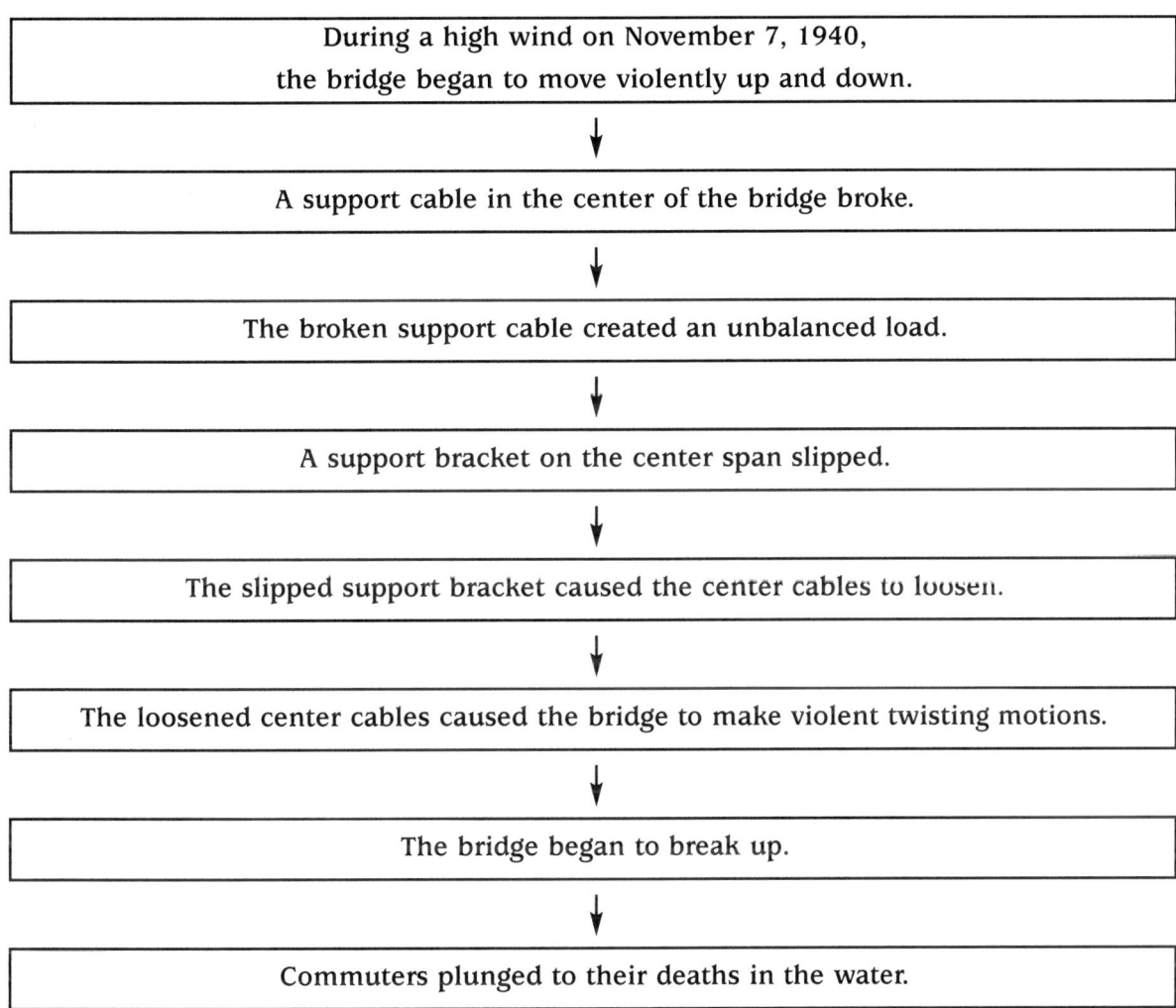

Discuss

Student Book p. 218

1. Answers will vary.
2. Answers will vary. Possible answers: Yes, engineers should be blamed when a bridge collapses. Engineers are supposed to receive an education and a professional license that qualifies them to build such things. People's lives depend on safe construction practices. Just as a doctor should not be allowed to continue practicing medicine if something goes wrong, so should an engineer be punished if faulty construction leads to the loss of human lives. **(OR)** No, engineers should not be blamed when a bridge collapses, unless there is strong evidence that they did something wrong. Unfortunately, some things are beyond their control. At times, nature is stronger than anything man can build. Should an engineer be blamed if an earthquake destroys a bridge, if they have done everything in their power to make it safe? We must remember that while safety is important, engineers generally do the best they can, and nature is more powerful.

Appendix I

Scanning Practice
Student Book p. 220

EXERCISE 1

1. *Sports Desk* is on at 8:00.
2. *Mercy General Hospital* is on channel 15 (UPN 38).
3. The topic of *Eyewitness to History* is the story of Hurricane Andrew.
4. A program that would be good for gardeners is *Plants for all Seasons*.
5. *All About Animals* is on Channel 2 at 8:30.

EXERCISE 2

1. The first bus leaves Woods Hole at 6:45.
2. Seven buses leave from Bourne on Sundays.
3. The last bus arrives at Logan Airport at 7:50.
4. The fare from Falmouth to Logan Airport is $22 one way, $40 round trip.
5. There are two stops in Wareham (Shore Road and Mills Road).
6. "X7" means that the bus does not operate on Saturdays or holidays, but it does run on Sundays.

EXERCISE 3

1. Professor Peack teaches Chemistry 155–01.
2. Chinese 301 meets on Mondays, Wednesdays, and Fridays from 10:00 A.M. to 10:50 A.M.
3. Biology 202 meets in the Chemistry Building, Room 123.
4. Computer Science 134 meets on Mondays, Wednesdays, and Fridays.
5. Astronomy 217–T1 meets in Clark Hall 204.
6. Professor Souza teaches Astronomy lab on Monday afternoon.

EXERCISE 4

1. Buttermilk pancakes (tall or short stacks) are served. Buttermilk pancakes are the basic type; bananas and berries can be added to or on top of the buttermilk pancakes.
2. A side order of bacon is $1.50.
3. The most expensive omelette is the vegetarian omelette, at $5.95.
4. Two eggs with ham, a small ("regular") apple juice, and a side order of sausage would cost $7.25
5. Answers may vary. Possible answers are: *scrambled, fried, fried over easy* or *sunny side up, poached*, and *omelettes*. "Any style" usually means types of *fried* eggs or *scrambled* eggs and sometimes *poached*.
6. There are two pancakes in a short stack and four pancakes in a tall stack.

EXERCISE 5

1. A room at the Pine Gardens Inn costs between $80 and $100 a night.
2. The Blain House has airport pick-up service.
3. The hotels that have kitchenettes are the Belvedere Hotel and the Pine Gardens Inn.
4. You can only watch television in the lounge at the Pine Gardens Inn, not in the rooms.
5. The hotels that offer Internet access are the Belvedere Hotel and Blain House.
6. You can go to a gym only at the Belvedere Hotel.

Skimming Practice
Student Book p. 225

1. b. Geography of the Great Plains
2. a. major cities in the Great Plains (Geographers traditionally study the face of the earth to map its physical characteristics, which can include naming animals or human life *native* to the land.)

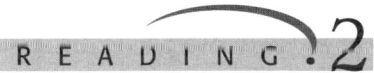

1. b. an article in *Vacationtime* magazine
2. c. water problems in Las Vegas

1. a. The Last Flight of Amelia Earhart
2. b. other famous people who have disappeared

1. c. a pamphlet on safety tips during severe weather
2. b. what to do in a snowstorm

Name: _____ Score: _____ out of 100

How Safe is Your Home?

A Guide to Fire Safety

Every year, more than 4,000 people in the United States die in residential fires—fires that start in the home. How can you be sure that your home and your family are safe from fire? Knowing about flammable products in your home is one way to start. Many people do not realize how the things they use every day can easily start a fire.

Cooking Equipment

Supplies used for cooking are responsible for around 100,000 fires, 400 deaths, and 5,000 injuries each year.

- Never place potholders, plastic utensils, or towels near a stove because high heat or flames can start a fire.
- Roll up long sleeves and don't reach across the stove while cooking. Long or loose sleeves can catch on fire. Also, they can catch on pot handles and cause burns.
- Do not place candy or cookies above stoves if small children are in the home. Children may try to climb onto the stove to reach them. Consequently, they could burn themselves if the stove is on, or start a fire by accidentally turning on the stove.

Furniture and Materials

Your home is filled with curtains, blankets, rugs, and furniture, all of which may be flammable.

- Always check furniture that a smoker has sat in. Lit cigarettes or cigarette ashes can fall behind or between cushions, or underneath furniture.
- Do not place or leave ashtrays on the arms of chairs, where they can fall or be knocked over.
- Move heaters or other fire sources at least three feet away from beds.

Clothing

Most clothing can burn. Some garments burn more quickly than others. Clothing usually catches fire because of small open flames, such as matches, cigarette lighters, and candles. The most flammable garments are pajamas, nightgowns, robes, shirts, pants, and dresses.

- Some clothing is labeled "flame resistant." That is, it is treated with a special chemical so it will not burn. These garments may require special care and cleaning. Read the labels carefully.
- Buy clothing made of fabrics such as 100% polyester, nylon, wool, and silk. These materials don't catch on fire easily. In contrast, fabrics such as cotton, cotton/polyester blends, rayon, and acrylic catch fire easily and burn rapidly.
- Buy clothing that can be removed easily, without having to be pulled over the head. Clothes that are easily removed can prevent serious burns if they catch fire.

Reading (65 points)

1. The title and subtitles suggest that this reading is probably about _____. (5 points)
   A. how to survive if your house catches fire
   B. how to avoid fires when you are cooking
   C. how to put out fires in the home
   D. how some things in the home can catch fire

2. Which question is answered in the article? (5 points)
   A. Who should you call if you have a fire in your kitchen?
   B. How far away should heaters or fire sources be from a bed?
   C. Where should you place the stove in your kitchen?
   D. How should you wash flame resistant clothing?

3. Which question is answered in the article? (5 points)
   A. What kind of furniture catches fire most often?
   B. Why isn't all clothing flame resistant?
   C. How many fires each year are caused by cooking equipment?
   D. How should you treat a burn?

4. Draw arrows from the underlined pronouns to their referents. Write an "X" over any without a referent. (20 points)
   A. Some clothing is labeled "flame resistant." That is, <u>it</u> is treated with a special chemical so it will not burn.
   B. Do not place candy or cookies above the stove if small children are in the home. Children may try to climb onto to the stove to reach <u>them</u>.
   C. Do not place or leave ashtrays on the arms of chairs, where <u>they</u> can fall or be knocked over.
   D. Clothes that are easily removed can prevent serious burns if they catch fire.

5. Read the following sentence. Underline the signal word. Then fill in the oval of the letter that best describes the purpose of the signal word. (10 points)

   Never place potholders, plastic utensils, or towels near a stove because high heat or flames can start a fire.

   The purpose of the signal word is to show _____.
   A. reason
   B. result
   C. example
   D. conclusion

142   QUIZ 1

6. Read the following sentences. Underline the signal word. Then fill in the oval of the letter that best describes the purpose of the signal word. (10 points)

  Long or loose sleeves can catch on fire. Also, they can catch on pot handles and cause burns.

  The purpose of the signal word is to show _____.

  A. contrast

  B. reason

  C. addition

  D. example

7. Which picture best illustrates the danger of fire in a kitchen? (10 points)

  A.

  B.

Vocabulary (35 points)

8. Read the following sentences. Only one of the underlined words is key to the main idea. Circle the word. (5 points)

    Buy clothing made of <u>fabrics</u> such as 100% polyester, <u>nylon</u>, wool, and silk. These materials don't catch on fire easily. In contrast, fabrics such as cotton, cotton/polyester <u>blends</u>, <u>rayon</u>, and <u>acrylic</u> catch fire easily and burn rapidly.

9. Read the following sentences. Only one of the underlined words is key to the main idea. Circle the word. (5 points)

    Clothing

    Most clothing can burn. Some <u>garments</u> burn more quickly than others. Clothing usually catches fire because of small open flames, such as matches, cigarette <u>lighters</u>, and candles. The most flammable garments are <u>pajamas</u>, nightgowns, <u>robes</u>, shirts, pants, and dresses.

10. Read the following sentences. Underline the internal definitions and circle the words they define. (25 points)

    A. Every year, more than 4,000 people in the United States die in residential fires—fires that start in the home.

    B. Buy clothing made of fabrics such as 100% polyester, nylon, wool, and silk. These materials don't catch on fire easily.

    C. Most clothing can burn. Some garments burn more quickly than others.

    D. Knowing about flammable products in your home is one way to start. Many people do not realize how the things they use every day can easily start a fire.

    E. Some clothing is labeled "flame resistant." That is, it is treated with a special chemical so it will not burn.

Name: _____ Score: _____ out of 100

www.hairtoheal.com

NEWS ONLINE

Archive | Classified | Shopping | promotions | Games | My news   news

Hair to Heal

Who Are We?

Hair to Heal is a nonprofit organization that makes wigs for kids under the age of 18. The custom-made hairpieces are made from donated hair. They are given to kids who have lost their hair because of medical treatment or illness.

The organization was started 15 years ago by Jessica Lowenthal, a former hairstylist and hair salon owner. When the daughter of a close friend lost her hair due to cancer treatments, Lowenthal saw the difference that a wig could make. The hair loss had caused a loss of self-esteem, but the wig helped to bring back the girl's confidence. She no longer felt shy about going back to school or seeing her friends. She no longer looked or felt different. "I realized that my friend's daughter had received more than a wig," says Lowenthal. "She got back a sense of herself. From that moment, I knew I wanted to start a company to give more children this gift."

Every year, Hair to Heal receives more than 1,000 hair donations and gives wigs to over 100 children.

How Does Hair to Heal Work?

Each week, Hair to Heal receives around 50 donations of hair. These are saved until a request comes for a hairpiece. Requests usually come from a hospital, a doctor, or a hair salon in the child's hometown. Then the hair is made into a wig, using the measurements and a photograph of the child's head. Finally, the wig is sent to the child.

Who Receives the Wigs?

The wigs mostly go to young cancer patients who have lost their hair due to chemotherapy. Others suffer from a medical condition called *alopecia areata*, which has no known cause or cure. *Alopecia areata* is a skin disease that leads to hair loss on the scalp and elsewhere on the body. Wigs are given to both boys and girls, but mostly to girls. This is because it is not as common for girls or young women to have no hair. It is not unusual, however, to see boys and young men with short, shaved, or no hair.

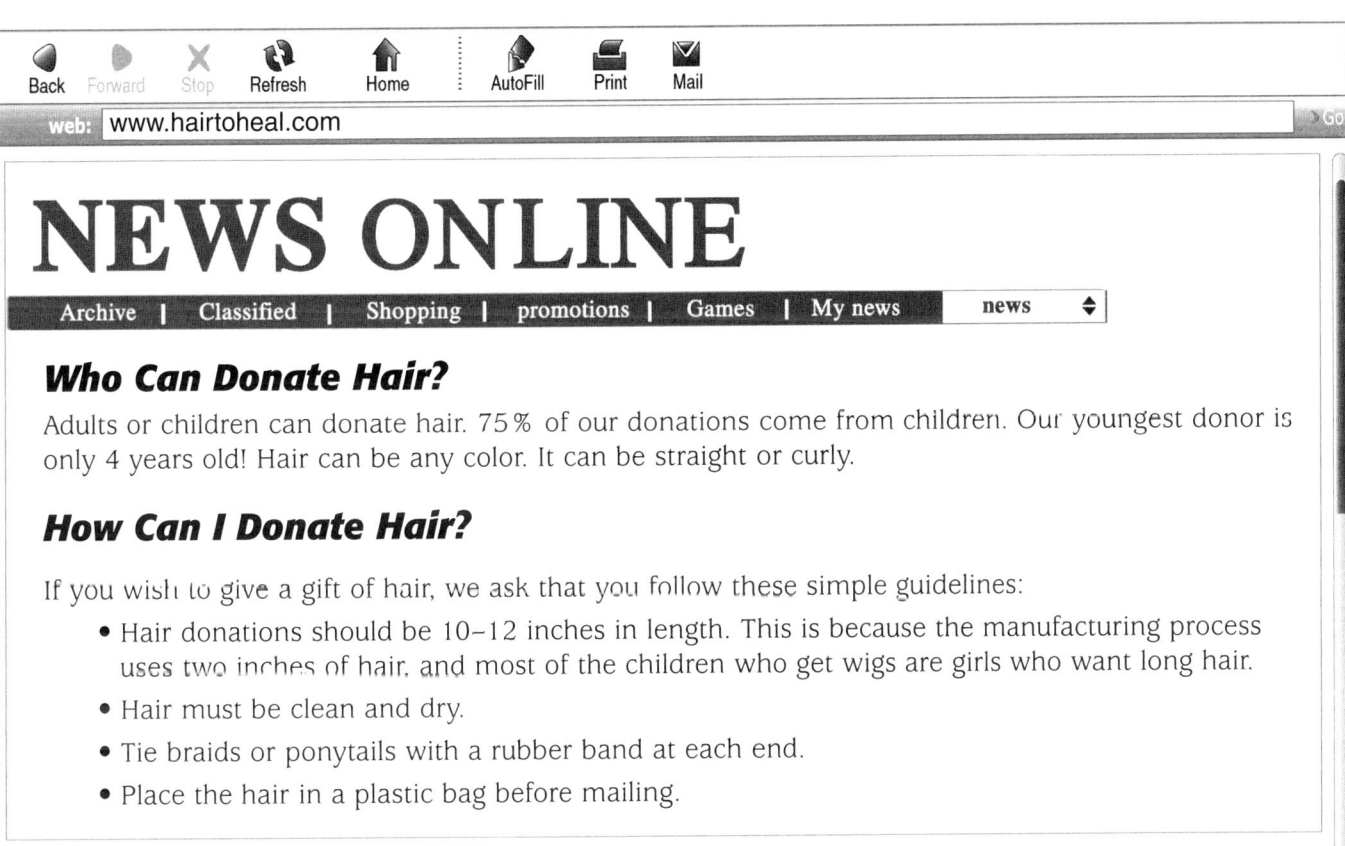

Reading (70 points)

1. The title and subtitles suggest that this reading is probably about _____. (5 points)
   A. children who have lost their hair
   B. a company that makes wigs for children who have lost their hair
   C. which diseases and medical treatments cause hair loss in children
   D. how wigs are made

2. Which question is NOT answered in the article? (5 points)
   A. How many children get Hair to Heal wigs each year?
   B. How many hair donors are children?
   C. How many hair donations does the company get each year?
   D. How many hair donors are male?

3. Which question is NOT answered in the article? (5 points)
   A. Why doesn't Hair to Heal help adults?
   B. Why do some children lose their hair?
   C. Why do wigs help children to heal?
   D. Why was Hair to Heal started?

4. Read the following passage. Then circle the letter that describes the best way to mark the passage. (5 points)

   How Does Hair to Heal Work?

   Each week, Hair to Heal receives around 50 donations of hair. These are saved until a request comes for a hairpiece. Requests usually come from a hospital, a doctor, or a hair salon in the child's hometown. Then the hair is made into a wig, using the measurements and a photograph of the child's head. Finally, the wig is sent to the child.

   What is the best way to mark this passage?

   A. Use exclamation points for opinions you agree with.
   B. Write notes in the margin where you don't agree.
   C. Number items in a process.
   D. Number reasons for something.

5. Draw arrows from the underlined pronouns to their referents. Write an "X" over any without a referent. (20 points)

   A. When the daughter of a close friend lost <u>her</u> hair as a result of cancer treatments, Lowenthal saw the difference that a wig could make.

   B. This is because <u>it</u> is not as common for girls or young women to have no hair.

   C. The custom-made hairpieces are given to kids who have lost <u>their</u> hair because of medical treatment or illness.

   D. "I realized that my friend's daughter had received more than a wig," says Lowenthal. "<u>She</u> got back a sense of herself."

6. Read the following sentence. Underline the signal word. Then fill in the oval the letter that best describes the purpose of the signal word. (10 points)

   Wigs are given to both boys and girls, but mostly to girls.

   The purpose of the signal word is to show _____.

   A. reason
   B. example
   C. contrast
   D. result

7. Read the following sentences. Underline the signal word. Then fill in the oval of the letter that best describes the purpose of the signal word. (10 points)

   Hair donations should be 10–12 inches in length. This is because the manufacturing process uses two inches of hair, and most the children who get wigs are girls who want long hair.

   The purpose of the signal word is to show _____.

   A. addition
   B. reason
   C. result
   D. example

8. Which picture best illustrates how to prepare a hair donation? (10 points)

A.   C.

 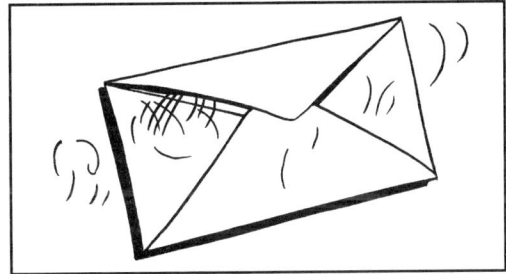

B.   D.

 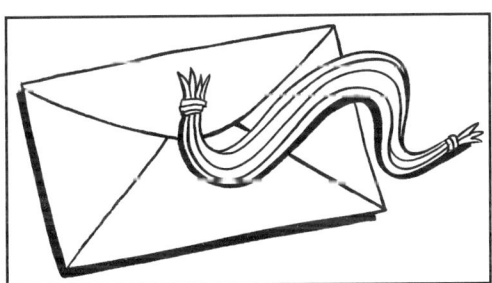

Vocabulary (30 points)

9. Complete the following sentences with the correct word form. (5 points)

   donate   donated   donations   donor

   A. Hair to Heal accepts _____ of clean, dry hair at least 10 inches long.
   B. A person who wishes to be a _____ can have any type of hair.
   C. If you wish to _____ hair, you can contact the organization for more information.
   D. All of the wigs are made with _____ hair, not with synthetic or artificial hair.

10. Read the following sentences. Underline the internal definition, and circle the words they define. (10 points)

    Others suffer from a medical condition called alopecia areata, which has no known cause or cure. Alopecia areata is a skin disease that leads to hair loss on the scalp and elsewhere on the body.

11. Read the following sentences. Underline the internal definition of the underlined word. Then fill in the oval of the letter that best describes the type of internal definition. (5 points)

    Hair to Heal is a nonprofit organization that makes <u>wigs</u> for kids under the age of 18. The custom-made hairpieces are made from donated hair.

    A. antonym   Ⓐ Ⓑ Ⓒ
    B. synonym
    C. restatement

12. Read the following sentences. Underline the internal definition of the underlined word. Then fill in the oval of the letter that best describes the type of internal definition. (5 points)

    How Can I <u>Donate</u> Hair?

    If you wish to give a gift of hair, we ask that you follow these simple guidelines:

    A. antonym
    B. synonym
    C. restatement

13. Read the following sentences. Underline the internal definition of the underlined word. Then fill in the oval of the letter that best describes the type of internal definition. (5 points)

    When the daughter of a close friend lost her hair due to cancer treatments, Lowenthal saw the difference that a wig could make. The hair loss had caused a loss of <u>self-esteem</u>, but the wig helped to bring back the girl's confidence.

    A. synonym
    B. restatement
    C. antonym

Name: _____   Score: _____ out of 100

Healthy Living Magazine

Ask Dr. Lee

Every month, our health editor, Dr. Yushen Lee, will answer your questions about health. This month, our topic is diet and nutrition.

Dear Dr. Lee,

I am a first-year college student. I also work part-time. I've been thin all my life, but I've noticed that I've gained some weight since school started—about ten pounds! I think the problem is that I eat more fast food than I used to. I'm so busy with classes and my part-time job that I usually don't have time to make food or to buy healthy food to bring for lunch. I'm always on the go—I'm busy from morning until night! I leave home at 7:00 in the morning and usually stop at Burger King for breakfast on my way to my 8:00 A.M. class. I can't afford to eat at expensive places. Most of the affordable places to eat around my college are fast-food places, so sometimes I eat at Wendy's for lunch. I usually have only a half hour to get to work after my afternoon classes, so I often go to Kentucky Fried Chicken for dinner. Do you think that my recent weight gain might be a result of eating at fast-food restaurants? Is there any way to eat healthy foods at fast-food restaurants? Please help! I don't want to be overweight.

—On the Go

Dear On the Go,

Fast-food restaurants serve food that is high in calories and high in fat. Restaurant food is calorie-dense, meaning that it has more calories per bite than the food you would probably eat at home. The portions are also very large. Most regular sized portions are larger than we need. Therefore, your recent weight gain is very likely a result of eating in fast-food restaurants so often. You should not eat three fast-food meals a day. You may gain energy from these meals for a short period of time, but your body is not getting all the nutrition it needs. You are putting your health in danger. However, eating in fast-food restaurants some of the time is okay. Just don't eat the high-calorie, high-fat foods. Consider the healthier alternatives.

Fast-food restaurants increasingly offer healthier choices. For instance, many fast-food restaurants now offer different types of salads, vegetables served in pita bread, or vegetables on the side. Instead of ordering a cheeseburger, large fries, and a soft drink, order a salad with chicken, a low-calorie dressing, and an iced tea or water. Avoid fried food; order food that is baked, broiled, steamed, roasted, or grilled. Watch out for sauces—these can contain surprisingly large amounts of calories and fat. Ask for sauces on the side, or skip them. Avoid cheese and mayonnaise. These items are very high in fat.

You should also watch your portions. A regular hamburger is almost four ounces and has 280 calories. That's not so bad. However, people don't usually eat a regular hamburger at a fast-food restaurant. A Big Mac weighs seven and a half ounces and has 590 calories! If you "super-size" your fries and buy a large soft drink, you could be eating a meal of over 1610 calories! That is close to the daily amount of calories required for a woman.

The chart below shows some healthy alternatives at fast-food restaurants and the amount of calories and fat in them. Consider keeping this chart in your wallet to remind yourself of these choices. Also remember that you can always ask the restaurants to give you a list of nutritional information about their menu.

Nutrition Chart: Healthy Fast-Food Alternatives

McDonald's	Calories	Fat (g)
Garden salad with fat-free vinaigrette dressing	135	6
Regular hamburger	280	10
Wendy's		
Small chili	210	7
Junior hamburger	270	9
Kentucky Fried Chicken		
Tender roast chicken sandwich (no sauce)	270	5
BBQ baked beans	190	3
Corn on the cob	150	1.5

Reading (75 points)

1. What audience is most likely to read this? (5 points)

   A. Doctors and nutrition experts
   B. Children
   C. General readers (teens and adults) interested in health
   D. Professionals who work in the fast-food industry

   Ⓐ Ⓑ Ⓒ Ⓓ

2. What is the purpose of the two letters? (5 points)

   A. To inform readers about how to make healthy choices in fast-food restaurants
   B. To persuade readers that eating in fast-food restaurants is dangerous
   C. To inform readers about which fast-food restaurants are the healthiest
   D. To give instructions on how to make healthier meals at home

   Ⓐ Ⓑ Ⓒ Ⓓ

3. In the letter from Dr. Lee (paragraph 3), which sentence is the topic sentence expressing the main idea? (5 points)

   A. For instance, many fast-food restaurants now offer different types of salads, vegetables served in pita bread, or vegetables on the side.
   B. Fast-food restaurants increasingly offer healthier choices.
   C. These items are very high in fat.
   D. Watch out for sauces—these can contain surprisingly large amounts of calories and fat.

   Ⓐ Ⓑ Ⓒ Ⓓ

4. In the letter from Dr. Lee (paragraph 4), which sentence is the topic sentence expressing the main idea? (5 points)

   A. A regular hamburger is almost four ounces and has 280 calories.
   B. However, people don't usually eat a regular hamburger at a fast-food restaurant.
   C. You should also watch your portions.
   D. That is close to the daily amount of calories required for a woman.

   Ⓐ Ⓑ Ⓒ Ⓓ

5. According to the nutrition chart, which menu item is the lowest in calories? (5 points)

   A. Corn on the cob
   B. Junior hamburger
   C. Tender roast chicken sandwich
   D. Garden salad with fat-free vinaigrette dressing

   Ⓐ Ⓑ Ⓒ Ⓓ

6. According to the nutrition chart, which menu item is the highest in fat? (5 points)

   A. Small chili
   B. Regular hamburger
   C. Tender roast chicken sandwich
   D. Junior hamburger

   Ⓐ Ⓑ Ⓒ Ⓓ

7. Draw arrows from the underlined pronouns, demonstrative pronouns, and adverbs to their referents. Write an "X" over any without a referent. (20 points)

   A. Watch out for sauces—these can contain surprisingly large amounts of calories and fat.
   B. If you "super-size" your fries and buy a large soft drink, you could be eating a meal of over 1610 calories! That is close to the daily amount of calories required for a woman.
   C. Also remember that you can always ask the restaurants to give you a list of nutritional information about their menu.
   D. The chart below shows some healthy alternatives at fast-food restaurants and the amount of calories and fat in them.

8. Read the following sentences. Underline the signal word. Then fill in the oval of the letter that best describes the purpose of the signal word. (10 points)

   Most regular-sized portions are larger than we need. Therefore, your recent weight gain is very likely a result of eating in fast-food restaurants so often.

   The purpose of the signal word is to show _____.

   A. addition
   B. contrast
   C. order
   D. effect

   Ⓐ Ⓑ Ⓒ Ⓓ

152 QUIZ 3

9. Read the following sentence. Underline the signal word. Then fill in the oval of the letter that best describes the purpose of the signal word. (10 points)

   Instead of ordering a cheeseburger, large fries, and a soft drink, order a salad with chicken, a low-calorie dressing, and an iced tea or water.

The purpose of the signal word is to show _____.

   A. contrast
   B. order
   C. addition
   D. example

   Ⓐ Ⓑ Ⓒ Ⓓ

10. Which graphic organizer would best illustrate the problem stated in the letter written by "On the Go"? (5 points)

    A. Cluster diagram
    B. Flow chart
    C. Block diagram
    D. Timeline

    Ⓐ Ⓑ Ⓒ Ⓓ

Vocabulary (25 points)

11. Read the following list of words. Use the suffixes/word form to determine the part of speech. Then write the words in the chart. (5 points)

    afford   alternatives   nutrition   overweight   weigh
    affordable   items   nutritional   regular-sized   weight

Nouns	Verbs	Adjectives

12. Read the following sentences. Underline the internal definitions, synonyms, antonyms, or restatements and circle the words they define. (20 points)

    A. Food is calorie-dense, meaning that it has more calories per bite than the food you would probably eat at home.
    B. The chart below shows some healthy alternatives at fast-food restaurants and the amount of calories and fat in them. Consider keeping this chart in your wallet to remind yourself of these choices.
    C. I'm always on the go—I'm busy from morning until night!
    D. I can't afford to eat at expensive places. Most of the affordable places to eat around my college are fast-food places, so sometimes I eat at Wendy's for lunch.

Name: _____   Score: _____ out of 100

A Subterranean Tour: Seattle's Underground City

One of Seattle's favorite attractions is Bill Spiedel's Underground Tour. This 90-minute guided tour takes you beneath the streets of Pioneer Square to explore a historic section of the city. Unoccupied since 1907, this city below a city is now only old storefronts and empty buildings. None of them are used. Because there is no sunlight down there, this underground city feels more like a cave. This tour is an exciting and adventurous way to learn about the city's unusual history.

History

Before Seattle was a city, in the 1800s, the area was covered in water. The only land was a small island. It was terrible land for building. Most of it was mud. Then in 1852, settlers moved dirt to create more land on the island. They made the island a peninsula. The city was named "Seattle," after an Indian chief, and it quickly grew.

Unfortunately, problems resulted when the city was built. For instance, water from Puget Sound frequently flooded the streets. Also, wagon wheels made large holes in the muddy streets. The holes then filled with water. In the late 1800s, a 10-year-old boy died when he tried to cross a busy intersection. He fell into a hole that was 12 feet wide and eight feet deep. In addition, there were plumbing problems. Twice a day, all the toilets overflowed. This happened when the tides came in. The newspapers published schedules of the tides and told people when to flush their toilets.

Then in 1889, a terrible fire burned the entire city to the ground in 12 hours. The people of Seattle decided to rebuild the city 8 to 32 feet higher. However, they decided it would take too much time to move more dirt to make the streets higher. Therefore, they constructed the new buildings first. After that, they started filling in the streets with dirt. However, when they raised the level of the streets, they found a new problem: the first level of the buildings, including the storefronts and doors, would now be below the new street level. To solve that problem, they raised the streets but not the sidewalks.

Raising the street level was some improvement. The flooding and plumbing problems ended. However, other problems resulted. After leaving a shop, people had to climb up stairs or ladders to reach the street level. They had to cross the raised street and go down a ladder again to the sidewalk level on the other side. People often fell off the streets and onto the sidewalks. At least 17 people died this way.

When the Alaskan gold rush brought more than $100 million into the city, sidewalks were finally built at the raised street level. The old storefront doors were now below ground. The underground city was forgotten until 1965, when a local historian decided to start giving tours of it.

Touring the Underground City

The tour begins at historic Pioneer Square, where buildings from the 19th century stand on the original site of the city. First, you will go to Doc Maynard's, where your guide will tell you about the city's history. Next, your guide will take you below ground and lead you along the old sidewalks. You'll see old storefronts, doorways, windows, sidewalks, and building signs. Watch out—you might see some rats, too!

> The tour lasts 90 minutes. Wear comfortable walking shoes. Admission is $10.00 for adults, $8.00 for seniors and students, $5.00 for children 7-12. Admission is free for children under 7. Tours operate daily, year-round, although the schedule may change from season to season. Please call for more tour information: (206) 682-4646.

Reading (70 points)

1. Where is this reading most likely from? (5 points)
   A. History textbook
   B. Tourist guidebook
   C. Newspaper
   D. Journal of history scholars

2. What is the main purpose of this reading? (5 points)
   A. To persuade people to travel to Seattle
   B. To give opinions about taking the underground tour
   C. To inform readers about a popular Seattle tourist attraction
   D. To inform people about problems that can result from poor city planning

3. Which question is NOT answered in the article? (5 points)
   A. What will you see on the underground tour?
   B. When was the city of Seattle built?
   C. How many people go on the Underground Tour?
   D. What caused part of the city to be buried underground?

4. In paragraph 3, which sentence is the topic sentence expressing the main idea? (5 points)
   A. In the late 1800s, a 10-year-old boy died when he tried to cross a busy intersection.
   B. For instance, water from Puget Sound frequently flooded the streets.
   C. Unfortunately, problems resulted when the city was built.
   D. Twice a day, all the toilets overflowed.

5. In paragraph 5, which sentence is the topic sentence expressing the main idea? (5 points)
   A. However, other problems resulted.
   B. Raising the street level was some improvement.
   C. After leaving a shop, people had to climb up stairs or ladders to reach the street level.
   D. The flooding and plumbing problems ended.

Reading (65 points)

6. Draw arrows from the underlined pronouns, demonstrative pronouns, and adverbs to their referents. Write an "X" over any without a referent. (20 points)

   A. The city was named "Seattle," after an Indian chief, and <u>it</u> quickly grew.

   B. However, when they raised the level of the streets, they found a new problem: the first level of the buildings, including the storefronts and doors, would now be below the new street level. To solve <u>that problem</u>, they raised the streets but not the sidewalks.

   C. People often fell off the streets and onto the sidewalks. At least 17 people died <u>this way</u>.

   D. However, they decided that <u>it</u> would take too much time to move more dirt to make the streets higher.

   E. The underground city was forgotten until 1965, when a local historian decided to start giving tours of <u>it</u>.

7. In the following sentences, circle the signal words that show time or order. Then put the events in the correct order. (15 points)

   _____ Then in 1852, settlers moved dirt to create more land on the island. They made the island a peninsula.

   _____ After that, they started filling in the streets with dirt.

   _____ Then in 1889, a terrible fire burned the entire city to the ground in 12 hours.

   _____ The Alaskan gold rush brought more than $100 million into the city.

   _____ Before Seattle was a city, in the 1800s, the area was covered in water.

   _____ A local historian decided to give tours of the underground city.

   _____ Unfortunately, problems resulted when the city was built.

   _____ The people of Seattle decided to rebuild the city 8 to 32 feet higher.

   _____ With this new money, sidewalks were built at the street level and the old city went below the ground.

   _____ First, they rebuilt the buildings.

8. Which two graphic organizers could be used to illustrate the "History" section? (5 points)

   A. Timeline or block diagram   Ⓐ Ⓑ Ⓒ Ⓓ
   B. Flow chart or timeline
   C. Timeline or cluster diagram
   D. Block diagram or cluster diagram

9. Which graphic organizer could be used to illustrate the section "Touring the Underground City"? (5 points)

   A. Block diagram   Ⓐ Ⓑ Ⓒ Ⓓ
   B. Cluster diagram
   C. Timeline
   D. Flow chart

156 QUIZ 4

Vocabulary (30 points)

10. Read the following list of words. Use the suffixes/word form to determine the part of speech. Then write the words in the chart. (10 points)

    adventurous   decided   historic   intersection   sidewalks
    comfortable   historian history   operate   tides

Nouns	Verbs	Adjectives

11. Underline the prefix of each word on the left. Then match the words on the left to their possible meanings (or synonyms) on the right. (10 points)

Word	Possible Meaning or Synonym
1. subterranean	a. not lived in; abandoned
2. unoccupied	b. not normal
3. rebuild	c. underground/below the earth
4. unusual	d. where two streets come together/meet
5. intersection	e. construct again

12. Read the following passage. Circle the underlined word that is the most important to know. (10 points)

    The tour begins at historic Pioneer Square, where buildings from the 19TH century stand on the original site of the city. First, you will go to Doc Maynard's, where your guide will tell you about the city's history. Next, your guide will take you below ground and lead you along the old sidewalks. You'll see old storefronts, doorways, windows, sidewalks, and building signs. Watch out—you might see some rats, too!

    The tour lasts 90 minutes. Wear comfortable walking shoes. Admission is $10.00 for adults, $8.00 for seniors and students, $5.00 for children 7–12. Admission is free for children under 7. Tours operate daily, year-round, although the schedule may change from season to season. Please call for more tour information: (206) 682-4646.

Name: _____ Score: _____ out of 100

Chapter 5

Learning from Spiders:

The Search for Synthetic Silk

While silkworms make a silk strong enough for use in fabrics, spider silk is even stronger than silkworm silk. Scientists are researching how to make artificial silk similar to that of spiders. In this chapter, you will learn how spiders make silk. You will also learn how humans are trying to make synthetic silk.

How Spiders Make Silk

Spiders have eight silk-making glands. These glands produce silk for different purposes, such as capturing prey or forming egg sacs. The silk that researchers hope to copy is the type used for *dragline threads*. Dragline threads are the strongest threads that spiders create. Spiders use *dragline silk* to make the frame for their webs. This form of silk is also what a spider uses to drop down from a web and to escape or to grab its prey.

Dragline silk is produced in a gland called the *ampullate gland*. Cells in this gland mix proteins into a water solution. This mixture is pushed through a funnel into a *spinning duct*. The water is then mostly removed as the mixture travels through another duct. The fluid that is created is called *spin dope*. The spin dope then moves through a tube. At this point, some proteins form crystals. These protein crystals give the silk its strength. Finally, the silk is pulled into long threads by the spider's own weight or by the spider's back legs. The stretching process forces the protein crystals into a tightly woven mesh. This mesh forms the silk that is used for the spider's threads.

Artificial Spider Silk

Most people think of spider silk for its most common use: making webs. Few people think of spider silk for use in clothing—although in Paris in the 1700s, people wore gloves and stockings made from spider silk. However, scientists like the fiber for reasons other than beauty. Spider silk is extremely resilient; it is very hard to break. Besides being tough, spider silk is very elastic—it can stretch a lot without breaking. Finally, it is waterproof —water cannot hurt it. For these reasons, researchers have become interested in creating synthetic silk.

Imitation spider silk has many possible uses. It might be used to make stronger clothes, ropes, nets, and parachutes. It could also be used in the manufacture of medical supplies such as sutures and bandages. It could be used for bulletproof vests worn by soldiers and police officers. In fact, a bullet cannot go through clothing made of spider silk.

Manufacturing silk may seem like a lot of work. Silkworms can be farmed to produce large quantities of silk that can then be woven into fabrics. Why don't people farm spiders like silkworms? One reason is spiders are territorial—they do not like to share space. Spiders may even eat one another if they get too close. Therefore, scientists must find other ways to create a spider-like silk in large amounts. They want to create a synthetic fiber that will be as tough as natural spider silk, but easier to make and less expensive.

The next section will discuss recent developments in the research and manufacture of synthetic silk.

Reading (70 points)

1. What is this reading most likely from? (5 points)

   A. Magazine
   B. Textbook
   C. Brochure
   D. Newspaper

2. From the information provided in the first and last paragraphs, what is the main idea, or thesis, of this reading? (5 points)

   A. The process of making spider silk is very complicated.
   B. Many people think that only silkworms make silk.
   C. There have been some recent developments in making artificial silk.
   D. Spider silk is very strong, and researchers want to make something like it.

3. Which question is NOT answered in the reading? (5 points)

   A. How is spider silk made?
   B. How do researchers think synthetic silk could be used?
   C. How is synthetic silk made?
   D. How is spider silk different from silkworm silk?

4. Read the following sentences from paragraph 4. Which one expresses the main idea, or topic sentence, of the paragraph? (5 points)

   A. However, scientists like the fiber for reasons other than beauty.
   B. Spider silk is extremely resilient; it is very hard to break.
   C. For these reasons, researchers have become interested in creating synthetic silk.
   D. Most people think of spider silk for its most common use: making webs.

5. Read the following details from paragraph 4. Which detail is a description? (5 points)

   A. In Paris in the 1700s, people wore gloves and stockings made from spider silk.
   B. Besides being tough, spider silk is very elastic—it can stretch a lot without breaking.
   C. Few people think of spider silk for use in clothing.
   D. For these reasons, scientists have become interested in creating synthetic silk.

6. Read the following sentences. Write the word or phrase omitted at the ellipsis, indicated by the symbol Δ. Then underline the word or phrase it refers to. (20 points)

   A. Why don't people farm spiders like Δ silkworms?

   B. They want to create a synthetic fiber that will be as tough as natural spider silk, but Δ easier to make and less expensive.

   C. Finally, the silk is pulled into long threads by the spider's own weight or Δ by the spider's back legs.

   D. This form of silk is also what a spider uses to drop down from a web and escape or to Δ grab its prey.

7. Read the following sentences. Underline the signal word. Then fill in the oval of the letter that best describes the purpose of the signal word. (5 points).

   While silkworms make a silk strong enough for use in fabrics, spider silk is even stronger than silkworm silk. Scientists are researching how to make artificial silk similar to that of spiders.

   The purpose of the signal word is _____.

   A. to show time order
   B. to show addition
   C. to balance contrasting points
   D. to emphasize similar points

8. Read the following sentences. Underline the signal word. Then fill in the oval of the letter that best describes the purpose of the signal word. (5 points).

   It could be used for bulletproof vests worn by soldiers and police officers. In fact, a bullet cannot go through clothing made of spider silk.

   The purpose of the signal word is _____.

   A. to emphasize similar points
   B. to make something clear
   C. to balance contrasting points
   D. to show addition

9. Read the following passage. What inference can be made from this information? (5 points)

   Why don't people farm spiders like silkworms? One reason is spiders are territorial—they do not like to share space. Spiders may even eat one another if they get too close. Therefore, scientists must find other ways to create a spider-like silk in large amounts.

   A. Spiders don't like silkworms and may eat them.
   B. It is not possible to keep many spiders together in one place or to farm them for silk.
   C. Spiders do not produce as much silk as silkworms do.
   D. Spiders do not like to share space.

10. Which graphic organizer would best illustrate the section "How Spiders Make Silk"? (5 points)

    A. Timeline
    B. Cluster diagram
    C. Block diagram
    D. Flow chart

160 QUIZ 5

11. Choose the information that would best complete the outline of main sections of this reading. (5 points)

   I. How Spiders Make Silk
   II. The Search for a Synthetic Silk
   III. _____

   A. The Uses of Imitation Spider Silk
   B. Dragline Silk
   C. Recent Developments in the Research and Manufacture of Synthetic Silk
   D. Why Scientists Want to Create Synthetic Silk

Vocabulary (30 points)

12. Read the following sentences. Underline the internal definitions, synonyms, antonyms, restatements, or grouping clues. Circle the words they define. (20 points)

    A. Scientists are researching how to make artificial silk similar to that of spiders. In this chapter, you will learn how spiders make silk. You will also learn how humans are trying to make synthetic silk.
    B. Besides being tough, spider silk is very elastic—it can stretch a lot without breaking.
    C. It could also be used in the manufacture of medical supplies such as sutures and bandages.
    D. Spiders are territorial—they do not like to share space.
    E. Spider silk is extremely resilient; it is very hard to break.

13. Read the following sentences. Use context clues and the word form to choose the best dictionary definition to define the underlined word. (5 points)

    This mixture is pushed through a funnel into a *spinning duct*. The water is then mostly removed as the mixture travels through another duct.

    A. A tube or pipe inside a body, which carries fluids from glands
    B. A tube formed by cells in plant tissue
    C. A pipe for carrying an electric power line, telephone cables, or other conductors
    D. A layer (as in the atmosphere or the ocean) in which radio or sound waves are confined to a restricted path

14. Read the following sentences. Use context clues and the word form to choose the best dictionary definition to define the underlined word. (5 points)

    The stretching process forces the protein crystals into a tightly woven mesh. This mesh forms the silk that is used for the spider's threads.

    A. An arrangement of interlocking metal links, used especially for jewelry
    B. A network of threads or fibers, woven together with evenly spaced holes
    C. To catch in the openings of a net
    D. To fit or work together properly

Name: _____ Score: _____ out of 100

Letters to the Editor

Escape From Hollywood?

To the Editor:

I regularly read the movie reviews in the *Community Voice* newspaper. I've noticed that your newspaper favors major Hollywood movies; these are the only movies that are reviewed. You never review independent or foreign language films. According to the well-known film critic Robert Klein, movie reviews have a lot of power. They can bring people into movies or keep people out of them. Therefore, movie reviewers should pay more attention to "smaller" movies that don't have a lot of money for advertising.

Hollywood films are mostly interested in making money. Movies get made if somebody thinks they have commercial value—that is, if they can sell. It costs at least $55 million to make a Hollywood movie, and another $25 million to sell it. Commercial success usually depends on hiring famous actors. For instance, Tom Hanks and Julia Roberts attract large audiences—and also multi-million dollar salaries. Commercial success also depends on "standard" stories and conventional, predictable subjects—in other words, "safe" topics. Hollywood studios don't want to offend anyone and lose money. Hollywood movies are run by corporations, not by artists. Look at all the merchandise such as books, toys, video games, CDs, posters, and T-shirts that comes out with most Hollywood movies.

While many Hollywood movies are entertaining and fun to see, most are not. Too often they show a lot of violence. Or they are boring because they are all alike—I almost fell asleep at one last week. I did, however, see one amazing Hollywood film last year about a teacher who inspired some troubled students. That was a great movie because it teaches an important lesson.

Independent and foreign language films, on the other hand, are usually more interested in making art. They are made for very little money—sometimes for as little as $30,000. Without financial support, filmmakers often pay for their films themselves. Also, instead of relying on expensive special effects, these films try to teach us something or to make us see something different—a different way of thinking, or a different culture. Finally, independent and foreign films often make movies about difficult subjects.

Without a lot of financial support, these smaller and foreign language films depend on other kinds of publicity to sell tickets. Movie reviewers have the power to create publicity for any film. Your newspaper should review different types of movies, not just ones that make a lot of money and are "popular."

—Timothy Rossa
Boston, MA

Send letters to: The Editor, *Boston Community Voice*, 111 State St., Bldg. 2, 5th floor, Boston, MA 02109.

162 QUIZ 6

Reading (70 points)

1. What is the main purpose of this reading? (5 points)

    A. To inform people about Hollywood and independent/foreign films
    B. To give an opinion about Hollywood and independent/foreign films
    C. To give instructions about where to see independent/foreign films
    D. To describe the history of the film industry

    Ⓐ Ⓑ Ⓒ Ⓓ

2. From the information provided in the first and last paragraphs, what is the main idea, or thesis, of this reading? (5 points)

    A. Movie reviewers should pay more attention to "smaller" movies that don't have a lot of money for advertising.
    B. You never review independent or foreign language films.
    C. According to the well-known film critic Robert Klein, movie reviews have a lot of power.
    D. I regularly read the movie reviews in the *Community Voice* newspaper.

    Ⓐ Ⓑ Ⓒ Ⓓ

3. Which question is answered in the reading? (5 points)

    A. What are some good independent and foreign films that people should see?
    B. What are some Hollywood films that people should not see?
    C. Why are Hollywood studios more interested in making money than in making art?
    D. What happens if a Hollywood movie does not make a lot of money?

    Ⓐ Ⓑ Ⓒ Ⓓ

4. Read the following supporting details from paragraphs 2 and 3. Match the details on the left to the types of details on the right. (5 points)

Supporting Detail	Type of Supporting Detail
1. It costs at least $55 million to make a Hollywood movie, and another $25 million to sell it.	a. Example
2. According to the well-known film critic Robert Klein, movie reviews have a lot of power. They can bring people into movies or keep people out of them.	b. Fact
3. For instance, Tom Hanks and Julia Roberts attract large audiences—and also multi-million dollar salaries.	c. Statistic
4. Without financial support, filmmakers often pay for their films themselves.	d. Expert

5. Read and evaluate the following supporting detail from paragraph 3. (5 points)

   Or they are boring because they are all alike—I almost fell asleep at one last week.

   This detail _____.

   A. shows strong support for the topic
   B. shows weak support for the topic
   C. does not support the topic
   D. supports the opposite side of the topic

   Ⓐ Ⓑ Ⓒ Ⓓ

6. Read and evaluate the following supporting detail from paragraph 3. (5 points)

   I did, however, see one amazing Hollywood film last year about a teacher who inspired some troubled students. That was a great movie because it teaches an important lesson.

   This detail _____.

   A. shows strong support for the topic
   B. shows weak support for the topic
   C. does not support the topic
   D. supports the opposite side of the topic

   Ⓐ Ⓑ Ⓒ Ⓓ

7. Read the following sentences. Write the word or phrase omitted at the ellipsis, indicated by the symbol Δ. Then underline the word or phrase it refers to. (20 points)

   A. It costs at least $55 million to make a Hollywood movie, and Δ another $25 million to sell it.
   B. Commercial success also depends on "standard" stories and Δ conventional, predictable subjects—in other words, "safe" topics.
   C. Hollywood studios don't want to offend anyone and Δ lose money.
   D. They are made for very little money—sometimes Δ for as little as $30,000.

8. Read the following sentence. Underline the signal word. Then fill in the oval of the letter that best describes the purpose of the signal word. (5 points)

   Commercial success also depends on "standard" stories and conventional, predictable subjects—in other words, "safe" topics.

   The purpose of the signal word is _____.

   A. to make something clear
   B. to show addition
   C. to emphasize similar points
   D. to show contrast

   Ⓐ Ⓑ Ⓒ Ⓓ

9. Read the following passage. What inference can be made from this information? (5 points)

   Large movies get made if somebody thinks they have commercial value—that is, if they can sell. It costs at least $55 million to make a Hollywood movie and another $25 million to sell it. Commercial success usually depends on hiring famous actors.

   Independent and foreign films, on the other hand, are more interested in making art. They are made for very little money—sometimes for as little as $30,000.

   A. A major studio will never be interested in an independent film.
   B. Independent films almost never star famous actors.
   C. Actors in independent films will work for as little as $30,000.
   D. If a famous actor appears in an independent film, the film will definitely be a success.

   Ⓐ Ⓑ Ⓒ Ⓓ

164 QUIZ 6

10. Read the following passage. What inference can be made from this information? (5 points)

    Commercial success depends on "standard" stories and conventional, predictable subjects—in other words, "safe" topics. Hollywood studios don't want to offend anyone, and lose money.

    A. All Hollywood movies are happy.
    B. Hollywood studios prefer to deal with "safe" subjects.
    C. An independent film is more likely than a Hollywood movie to be about a difficult topic.
    D. Negative talk about a movie might actually increase ticket sales.

    Ⓐ Ⓑ Ⓒ Ⓓ

11. Complete the second part of the outline with the following information. (5 points)

    Are not as interested in making money
    are sometimes paid for by filmmakers themselves
    don't rely on expensive special effects
    may try to show us a different culture
    often make movies about difficult subjects
    often show violence
    usually need famous actors with high salaries
    usually try to teach us something

    ## Escape From Hollywood?

    I. Hollywood films
       A. Are interested in money
          1. must have commercial value
          2. cost at least $55 million to make, $25 million to sell
          3. _____
          4. studios are run by business people, not artists
          5. merchandise related to movies brings in more money
       B. Are less interested in art
          1. conventional, predictable, "safe"—don't want to offend
          2. don't usually try to teach us something
          3. _____

    II. Independent films
       A. _____
          1. are made for almost no money—as little as $30,000
          2. _____
          3. _____
       B. Are more interested in making art
          1. _____
          2. _____
          3. _____

QUIZ 6 **165**

Vocabulary (40 points)

12. Read the following list of words. Use the suffixes/word form to determine the part of speech. Then write the words in the chart. (10 points)

    artistic   conventional   financial   lose   reviewers
    commercial   depend   independent   merchandise   reviews

Nouns	Verbs	Adjectives

13. Read the following sentence. Underline the abbreviations and write what they abbreviate. (5 points)

    Send letters to: The Editor, *Boston Community Voice*, 111 State St., Bldg. 2, 5th floor, Boston, MA 02109.

14. Underline the signal words that show a grouping clue. Then use the grouping clue and your knowledge of word forms/parts of speech to choose the best meaning of the underlined word in the following sentence. (10 points)

    Look at all the <u>merchandise</u> such as books, toys, video games, CDs, posters, and T-shirts that comes out with most Hollywood movies.

    A. To sell things
    B. Things that are sold
    C. A person who sells things
    D. The money that people get from selling things

15. Read the following sentence. Use context clues and word form clues to choose the best dictionary definition to define the underlined word. (5 points)

    I've noticed that your newspaper <u>favors</u> major Hollywood movies; these are the only movies that are reviewed.

    A. Friendly or approving attention, especially by a superior
    B. Acts of kindness
    C. Small gifts given out at a party
    D. To show a preference for one thing as opposed to another

 Answer Keys

Reading
1. **D.** how some things in the home can catch fire
2. **B.** How far away should heaters or fire sources be from a bed?
3. **C.** How many fires each year are caused by cooking equipment?
4. Pronouns and their referents:
   A. it = (some) clothing/clothing labeled "flame resistant"
   B. them = candy or cookies
   C. they = ashtrays
   D. they = clothes
5. Signal word = *because*
   Purpose = **A.** to show reason
6. Signal word = *Also*
   Purpose = **C.** to show addition
7. **B.** is the best illustration to show fire dangers in a kitchen according to the article

Vocabulary
8. *fabrics* is the most important word (the word repeats, and synonyms/examples are given)
9. *garments* is the most important word (the word repeats, and synonyms/examples are given)
10. Internal definitions and the words they define:
    A. Internal definition = fires that start in the home
       Word it defines = residential fires
    B. Internal definition = synonym: materials; examples: polyester, nylon, wool, and silk
       Word it defines = fabrics
    C. Internal definition = synonym: clothing
       Word it defines = garments
    D. Internal definition = can easily start a fire
       Word it defines = flammable
    E. Internal definition = treated with a special chemical so it will not burn
       Word it defines = flame resistant

Reading
1. **B.** a company that makes wigs for children who have lost their hair
2. **D.** How many hair donors are male?
3. **A.** Why doesn't Hair to Heal help adults?
4. **C.** Number items in a process
5. Pronouns and their referents:
   A. her = the daughter of a close friend
   B. it = X (it is a subject pronoun here; no referent)
   C. their = kids
   D. She = my friend's daughter
6. Signal word = *but*
   Purpose = **C.** to show contrast
7. Signal word = *because*
   Purpose = **B.** to show reason
8. **A.** is the picture that best illustrates how to prepare hair for donation, according to the article.

Vocabulary
9. A. donations
   B. donor
   C. donate
   D. donated
10. Internal definition = a skin disease that leads to hair loss on the scalp and elsewhere on the body

166

QUIZ: Answer Keys

Word it defines = *alopecia areata*

11. Internal definition = hairpieces
    Type of internal definition = **B.** synonym
12. Internal definition = give a gift (of hair)
    Type of internal definition = **C.** restatement
13. Internal definition = confidence
    Type of internal definition = **A.** synonym

Reading

1. **C.** General readers (teens and adults) interested in health
2. **A.** To inform readers about how to make healthy choices in fast-food restaurants
3. **B.** Fast-food restaurants increasingly offer healthier choices.
4. **C.** You should also watch your portions.
5. **D.** Garden salad with fat-free vinaigrette dressing
6. **B.** Regular hamburger
7. Pronouns/adverbs and their referents:
   A. these = sauces
   D. that = 1610 calories
   C. that = X (head of a noun clause; no referent)
   D. them = healthy alternatives
8. Signal word = *Therefore*
   Purpose = **D.** to show effect or result
9. Signal word = *Instead (of)*
   Purpose = **A.** to show contrast
10. **B.** Flow chart

Vocabulary

11. The chart should be completed as follows:

Nouns	Verbs	Adjectives
alternatives	afford	affordable
items	weigh	nutritional
nutrition		overweight
weight		regular-sized

12. **A.** Internal definition – it has more calories per bite than the food you would probably eat at home
    Word it defines – calorie-dense
    B. Internal definition = synonym: choices
    Word it defines = alternatives
    C. Internal definition = I'm busy from morning until night!
    Word it defines = On the go
    E. Internal definition – antonym: expensive
    Word it defines = affordable

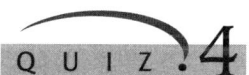

Reading

1. **B.** Tourist guidebook
2. **C.** to inform readers about a popular Seattle tourist attraction
3. **C.** How many people go on the Underground Tour?
4. **C.** Unfortunately, problems resulted when the city was built.
5. **A.** However, other problems resulted.
6. Pronouns and their referents:
   A. it = the city

# Answer Keys

B. that problem = the first level of the buildings would now be below the new street level

C. this way = falling off the streets and onto the sidewalk

D. it = X (subject pronoun; no referent)

E. it = the underground city

7. The signal words that should be circled appear in boldface.

__2__ **Then** in 1852, settlers moved dirt to create more land on the island. They made the island a peninsula.

__7__ **After that**, they started filling in the streets with dirt.

__4__ **Then** in 1889, a terrible fire burned the entire city to the ground in 12 hours.

__8__ The Alaskan gold rush brought more than $100 million into the city.

__1__ **Before** Seattle was a city, in the 1800s, the area was covered in water.

__10__ A local historian decided to give tours of the underground city.

__3__ Unfortunately, flooding and plumbing problems resulted.

__5__ The people of Seattle decided to rebuild the city 8 to 32 feet higher.

__9__ With this new money, sidewalks were built at the street level and the old city went below the ground.

__6__ **First,** they rebuilt the buildings.

8. **A.** Timeline or block diagram
9. **B.** Cluster diagram

Vocabulary

10. The chart should be completed as follows:

Nouns	Verbs	Adjectives
intersection	decided	adventurous
historian	operate	historic
history		comfortable
sidewalks		
tides		

11. The prefixes that should be underlined appear in boldface.
    1. c. **sub**terranean (sub = below, under)
    2. a. **un**occupied (un = not)
    3. e. **re**build (re = again)
    4. b. **un**usual (un = not)
    5. d. **inter**section (inter = together)
12. The word historic should be circled. It is the most important word to know because it repeats in another word form.

Reading

1. **B.** Textbook
2. **D.** Spider silk is very strong, and researchers want to make something like it.
3. **C.** How is synthetic silk made?
4. **A.** However, scientists like the fiber for reasons other than beauty.
5. **D.** Besides being tough, spider silk is very elastic—it can stretch a lot without breaking.
6. The omitted words that fill in the ellipsis appear in boldface. They connect to the underlined words.

    A. Why don't <u>people farm</u> spiders like **people farm** silkworms?

168

B. They want to create a synthetic fiber that will be as tough as natural spider silk, but **(to create a synthetic fiber) that will be** easier to make and less expensive.

C. Finally, the silk is pulled into long threads by the spider's own weight or **the silk is pulled into long threads** by the spider's back legs.

D. This form of silk is also what a spider uses to drop down from a web and escape or **What a Spider uses** to grab its prey.

7. Signal word = *while*
   Purpose = C. to balance contrasting points
8. Signal word = *In fact*
   Purpose = A. to emphasize similar points
9. B. It is not possible to keep many spiders together in one place or to farm them for silk.
10. D. Flow chart
11. C. Recent Developments in the Research and Manufacture of Synthetic Silk

Vocabulary

12. C. Internal definition = synonym: artificial
    Word it defines = synthetic

    B. Internal definition = restatement: it can stretch a lot without breaking
    Word it defines = elastic

    C. Internal definition = grouping clue: medical supplies
    Word it defines = sutures and bandages

    D. Internal definition = restatement: do not like to share space
    Word it defines = territorial

    E. Internal definition = it is very hard to break
    Word it defines = resilient

13. A. A tube or pipe inside a body, which carries fluids from glands
14. B. A woven material of threads or fibers, with evenly spaced holes

Reading

1. B. To give an opinion about Hollywood and independent/foreign films
2. A. Movie reviewers should pay more attention to "smaller" movies that don't have a lot of money for advertising.
3. C. Why are Hollywood studios more interested in making money than in making art?
4. Details and types of details (matching):
   1. c. statistic
   2. d. expert
   3. a. example
   4. b. fact
5. B. Shows weak support for the topic
6. D. Supports the opposite side of the topic
7. The omitted words that fill in the ellipsis appear in boldface. They connect to the underlined words.

   A. It costs at least $55 million to make a Hollywood movie, and **it costs** another $25 million to sell it.

   B. Commercial success also depends on "standard" stories and **commercial success depends on** conventional, predictable subjects—in other words, "safe" topics.

   C. Hollywood studios don't want to offend anyone and **(Hollywood studios) don't want to** lose money.

   D. They are made for very little money—sometimes **they are made** for as little as $30,000.

8. Signal word = *in other words*
   Purpose = A. To make something clear
9. B. Independent films almost never star famous actors.
10. C. An independent film is more likely than a Hollywood movie to be about a difficult topic.

169

Answer Keys

11. The outline should be completed as follows:

    Escape From Hollywood?

    I. Hollywood films

    A. Are interested in money

    1. must have commercial value
    2. cost at least $55 million to make, $25 million to sell
    3. usually need famous actors with high salaries
    4. studios are run by businesspeople, not artists
    5. merchandise related to movies brings in more money

    B. Are less interested in art

    1. are conventional, predictable, "safe"—don't want to offend
    2. don't usually try to teach us something
    3. often show violence

    II. Independent films

    A. Are not as interested in making money

    1. are made for almost no money—as little as $30,000
    2. are sometimes paid for by filmmakers themselves
    3. don't rely on expensive special effects

    B. Are more interested in making art

    1. often make movies about difficult subjects
    2. usually try to teach us something
    3. may try to show us a different culture

Vocabulary

12. The chart should be completed as follows:

Nouns	Verbs	Adjectives
merchandise	depend	artistic
reviewers	lose	commercial
reviews		conventional
		financial
		independent

13. Abbreviations that should be underlined: St. (Street), Bldg. (Building), MA (Massachusetts)

14. Signal word = *such as*
    Purpose = **B.** Things that are sold

15. **D.** To show a preference for one thing as opposed to another

170